Coaching the Empty Backfield Offense

Joe W. Gilliam, Sr.

ISBN: 1-58518-886-7
Library of Congress Control Number: 2004100336
Cover design: Jeanne Hamilton
Text design: Jeanne Hamilton
Diagrams: Deborah Oldenburg
Front cover photo: Matt Stroshane/Getty Images

Coaches Choice
P.O. Box 1828
Monterey, CA 93942
www.coacheschoice.com

Dedication

To the late, great, John Ayers Merritt, a college football Hall-of-Famer; a Jackson State University Hall-of-Famer; and a Tennessee State Hall-of-Famer with whom I worked twenty-four years. I thank him for his patience, and for allowing me the coaching latitude that enabled me to grow. He has my unwavering gratitude.

To the offensive players I coached at Jackson State University and Tennessee State University. I learned a great deal about football and about young people from them. To all those young men, I extend my sincere thanks.

Acknowledgments

I embarked upon my love of football at Grant Junior High School, in my hometown of Steubenville, Ohio. My first football coach was Angelo Vaccaro, and in high school, coaches Howard Brinker and William Ellis. I credit these three men with having planted the seed of football that continues to germinate and flower within me.

My collegiate years were interspersed with marriage, starting a family, and World War II. Initially at Indiana University, I was introduced to the rigors of Big Ten football under the helm of Alvin "Bo" McMillan. After that initial season when I.U. was voted "Mythical National NCAA Champions," I volunteered to serve in the Armed Forces. Next was West Virginia State College in Institute, West Virginia, where I played under Mark Hanna Caldwell. It was with Coach Caldwell that I began my apprenticeship in the study of offensive football.

I attended graduate school at the University of Kentucky, where I came into contact with the legendary coaches Blanton Collier and Homer Rice. In my estimation, these two individuals have always been among the brightest minds in the history of the game.

A tremendous debt of gratitude is owed all of the aforementioned gentlemen. For their patience and willingness to share their knowledge of the game that has brought me great challenge, satisfaction, and ultimately, my livelihood—I thank them all.

Finally, I want to thank my daughter, Kimberly Michelle Grant, for helping me to put words together in a manner that readers can understand.

Last, I am eternally grateful to Hi Lewis, former Vanderbilt University quarterback, who assisted with the typing and diagramming of the plays in this book.

Contents

Preface

I was initiated into the game of football in a little steel mill town on the Ohio River by the name of Steubenville, Ohio. It was there, at one of only two high schools in town, that I played tailback. At "Big Red," as our school was called, the tailback duties were, in many ways, similar to that of today's quarterback. The tailback did most of the running, nearly all of the passing, and, in most instances, he called the plays. He was positioned three-and-a-half yards directly behind the center and took most of the direct snaps. Reflecting back on my offensive football experience, I began to see a trend develop. While at Indiana University, we used what was called the "Cockeyed T-Formation." Again, the duties of the tailback were similar, in this case much like that of the single wing offense.

With the empty backfield offense, I saw the trend come full circle. Like the tailback many years ago at Steubenville's Big Red High School, the tailback in this offensive scheme has duties typically associated with those of the quarterback.

Back at Big Red, our offense came to us by way of Coach Howard Brinker, who learned it from Paul Brown of the Massillon, Ohio Tigers, the Cleveland Browns, and the Cincinnati Bengals. It was these two men, along with the late Alvin "Bo" McCallister of Indiana University, who began the stirrings of what has become the empty backfield offense.

Introduction

The idea for this book came to me while writing my previous work, *Coaching Football's Multiple Formations Offense*, published in 2000 by Coaches Choice. The term "empty backfield," the concept on which this current book is based, is mentioned in my earlier work, yet not in any significant detail. Nevertheless, this book will occasionally refer to entire sections of text contained in my 2000 work. Please forgive what may seem to be a less-than-creative device, but as the concept of the empty backfield unfolds, the reader will be able to discern the necessity of this decision.

A constant struggle exists in definition and design between offensive and defensive schemes. Offensive or defensive strategists will introduce a scheme, an alignment, or techniques that will force adjustments to the normal ways of doing "things." This creates the intellectual basis for the constantly evolving game of football—study, development, and adjustment—concepts that are integral to a comprehensive perception of the game. These concepts are constantly being revisited and re-evaluated in a vigilant effort to see the "big picture" as well as to answer each and every possible attack. I believe the empty backfield is an offensive scheme that forces existing defensive schemes to deviate from their "norms" in a very significant way. Up until now, defenses have only seen brief series of empty backfield schemes. However, as the reader will come to discover, the empty backfield proposed in the following pages is a complete offensive scheme of attack.

Legend

◯ = an offensive player

▢ = an offensive center

∿∿∿→ = a player going in motion or the direction of his movement

⟶ = the direct route of a player

● = the ballcarrier

⊤ = an offensive player blocking a defensive player

- - - →
LB = a direction of a player

T◯ ◯ = double-team and slip block

◯—⊣ = trap block

1

A Terrific Innovation In Offensive Football

The empty backfield offense features only one back aligned in the area from tackle to tackle. Normally, that one back is the quarterback. However, the quarterback can be exchanged, or interchanged, with a receiver/running back who is normally aligned in a slot or wing position.

The primary advantage of this offense is the ability to release four or five receivers immediately into the defensive secondary, thus forcing the defense to make significant adjustments. The defense will need to decide whether to defend against the pass by using increased numbers of pass defenders, or to blitz and leave receivers uncovered or leave defenders in man coverage. In either situation, the offense has a distinct advantage.

Seldom do most defenses see a team run an empty backfield offense for an entire game. The primary reason is because most offensive coaches have difficulty working out the blocking schemes, especially in the passing game. A common defensive approach to the infrequent empty backfield offense is to blitz. Thus, the empty backfield offense needs to account for all defensive linemen, as well as linebackers and secondary personnel in a potential blitz position.

When confronted with a possible eight-man pass rush, the offense needs to decide whether to block all outside rushers, or to utilize a "hot" receiver and throw before the outside rusher reaches the quarterback.

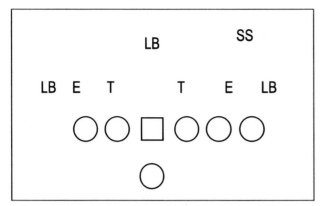

Note: 4-3 defensive alignment with the strong safety in a potential blitz position

Diagram 1-1a. Eight men in the box

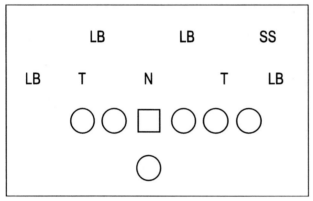

Note: 3-4 defensive alignment with the strong safety in a potential blitz position

Diagram 1-1b. Eight men in the box

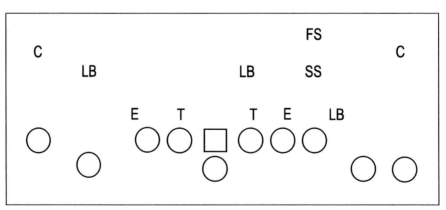

Diagram 1-2a. Strong safety in blitz position

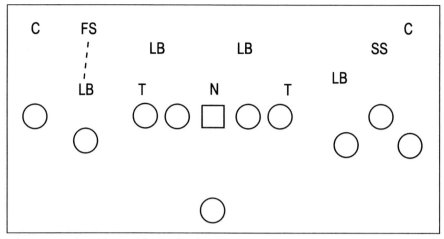

Diagram 1-2b. Left outside linebacker in blitz position

However, the empty backfield poses a three-fold challenge to these blitzing defenders:

If one or more linebackers and/or defensive backs choose to blitz, they will be vulnerable to the "hot" pass, or a pass route into their normal assigned areas. (Diagrams 1-3a and 1-3b)

If one or more linebackers choose not to blitz, they must become pass defenders, thereby being "mismatched" with wide receivers. (Diagrams 1-4a and 1-4b)

If the defense chooses to substitute defensive backs for one or more linebackers, they will probably weaken their run defense to some degree. (Diagrams 1-5a and 1-5b)

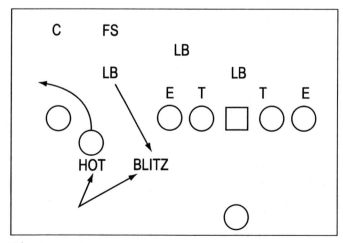

Diagram 1-3a.

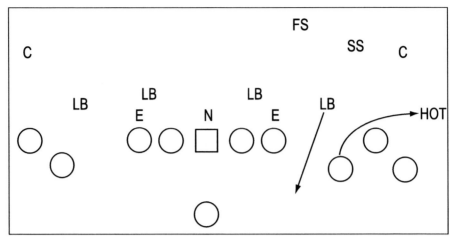

Diagram 1-3b.

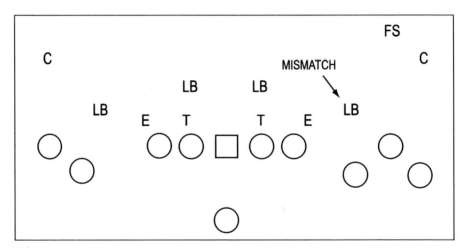

Diagram 1-4a.

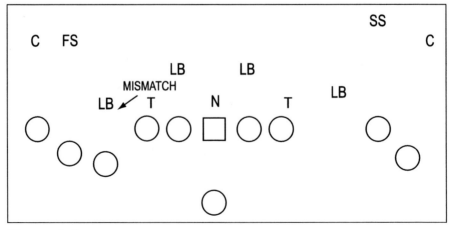

Diagram 1-4b.

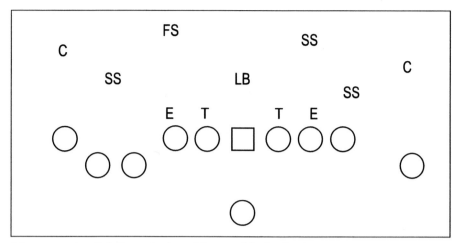

Diagram 1-5a. Safeties substituted for outside linebackers

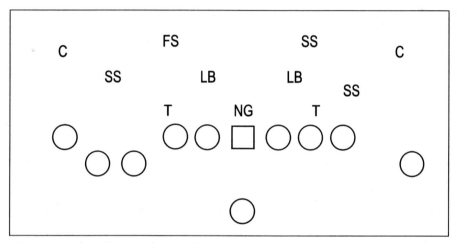

Diagram 1-5b. Safeties substituted for outside linebackers

In any of these three situations, the empty backfield offense remains one step ahead of the defense. To further complicate defensive adjustments, the empty backfield offense can shift into a variety of alignments and/or add motion before snapping the ball.

Further advantages of using the empty backfield offense include:

- It dictates the number of defenders committed to the run and the number committed to the pass.

- It encourages blitzing, thereby leaving coverages short-handed.

- It presents a scheme the defense usually only sees for a play or two.

- It places awesome pressure on linebackers and defensive backs.

- It allows the offense more opportunities to counter defensive schemes and adjustments.

- It increases scoring possibilities.

- The versatility of the scheme increases the excitement of the offensive players and thus initiates greater interest from players.

- It creates greater spectator interest by being wide open and unpredictable.

- When in the shotgun position, the quarterback has a better view of the pass rushers and the blitzers.

- Someone other than the quarterback can man the "shotgun" position.

- If a defensive coach uses a 4-3-4; 4-3 twin; 4-4-3; 6-1-4; 6-3-2; 3-4-4; 3-4 twin; or 3-5-3, he would either be outmanned in the secondary or have a linebacker committed to covering a wide receiver or tight end. It is not ideal to have defensive backs doing the work of linebackers against the run. Likewise, it is not ideal to have linebackers doing the work of defensive backs against the pass.

2

The Empty Backfield Offensive System

The numbering system of the empty backfield offense is the same as that of the multiple formation offense. The versatility of the empty backfield offense stems from its numbering system. The numbering of offensive holes and players is explained as follows:

- All offensive holes are mirrored, i.e. the same holes can be found on both sides of the center. The numbers of the holes on the right side of the center are even, single-digit numbers (2-4-6-8). The numbers on the left side of the center are odd, single-digit numbers (1-3-5-7). The number of the hole directly over the center is 0. The 0 hole is only in existence when the center is not covered by a down lineman.

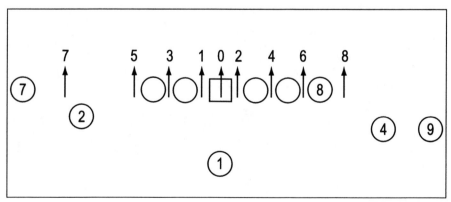

Diagram 2-1. Numbering of offensive holes and positions

- The tight end is number 8 and the split end is number 7. The flanker is number 9. The wing and slot receivers are numbers 2 and 4. This set-up allows for an endless variety of plays that can be numbered in an uncomplicated manner.

- Placing the number 1 behind the number of any running play converts that play into a play-action pass. Example: 47-1 means the 4 back fakes at the 7 hole.

The Receivers' Tree (Individual Routes of Receivers)

Since the various pass routes resemble the branches of a tree, it is appropriate to call all routes the "receivers' tree." These routes must be viewed as basic routes because receivers should be taught variations to these routes, depending on their read of defensive coverages. The numbering of the receivers' routes make possible a communication system with boundaries as limitless as double-digit combinations. Additionally, the language of the system becomes unmistakably clear. If a coach asks a receiver to run a "9" route, that receiver knows exactly what has been asked of him. As

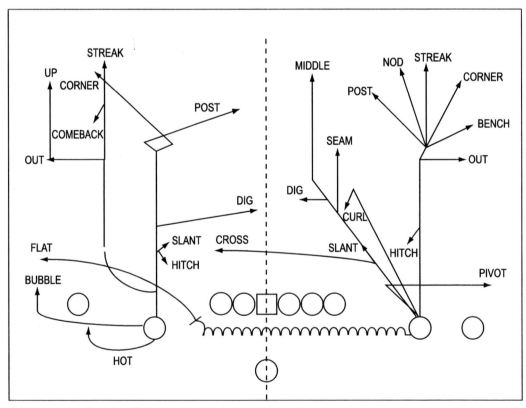

Diagram 2-2. Receivers' Tree

receivers practice the same routes, "running the tree," they become proficient at running those routes intrinsic to the system.

With the changing of offensive formations and pre-reads by the quarterback, the prospect of calling a different pass route through the use of audibles keeps each receiver alert on every play. The opponent probably does not know the meaning of the information that the quarterback has communicated to the receiver. Every receiver becomes a threat in the empty backfield offense. In the process, the possibility exists for the offense to give the defense the appearance of using many different patterns with minimal offensive difficulty. And the pass patterns can easily be designed to attack all of the passing zones.

Formations

In an effort to further complicate defensive assignments, the offense can start from an I-formation alignment or a split backfield alignment, and shift into the empty backfield alignment. Of course, different formations more readily facilitate certain kinds of plays.

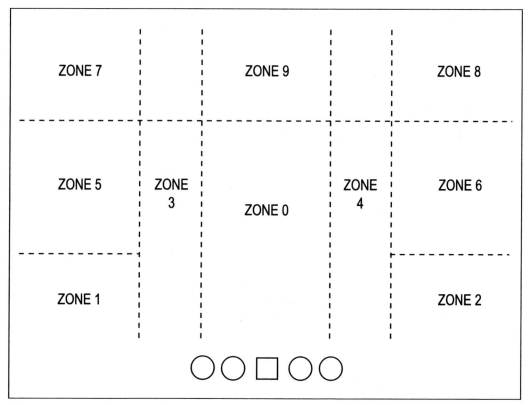

Diagram 2-3. Passing zone chart

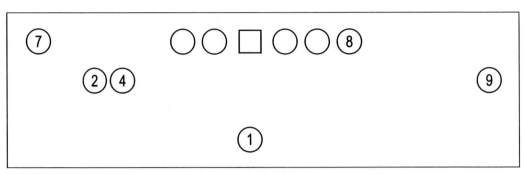

Diagram 2-4a. Formation 1: Pro right, double slot left

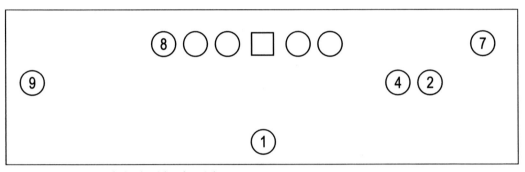

Diagram 2-4b. Pro left, double slot right

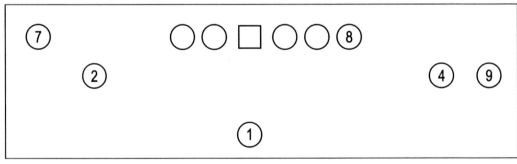

Diagram 2-4c. Formation 2: Pro right, trips right, slot left

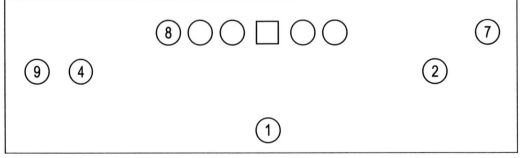

Diagram 2-4d. Pro left, trips left, slot right

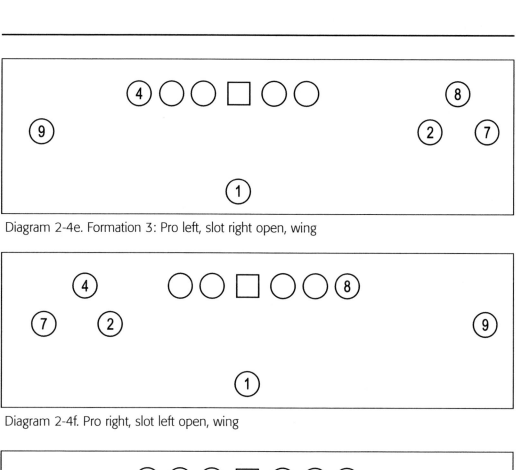

Diagram 2-4e. Formation 3: Pro left, slot right open, wing

Diagram 2-4f. Pro right, slot left open, wing

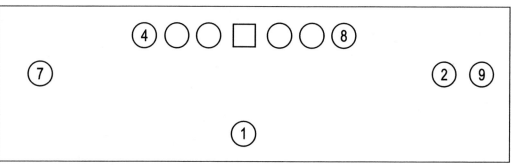

Diagram 2-4g. Formation 4: Double tight, wing right

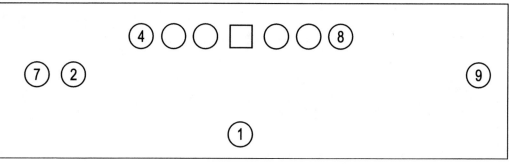

Diagram 2-4h. Double tight, wing left

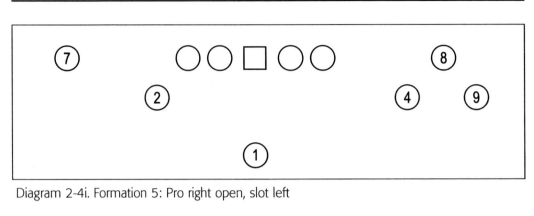

Diagram 2-4i. Formation 5: Pro right open, slot left

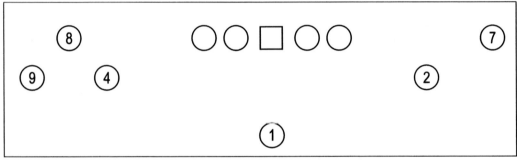

Diagram 2-4j. Pro left open, slot right

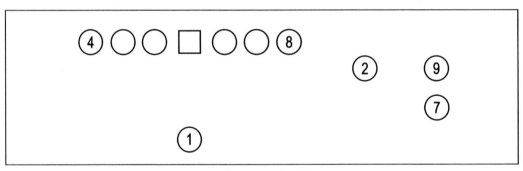

Diagram 2-4k. Formation 6: Pro right open, wing slot left

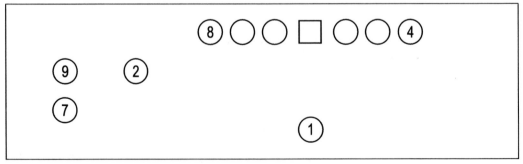

Diagram 2-4l. Pro left open, wing slot right

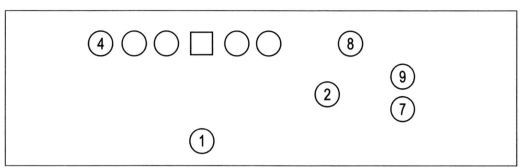

Diagram 2-4m. Formation 7: Double tight right, double wing

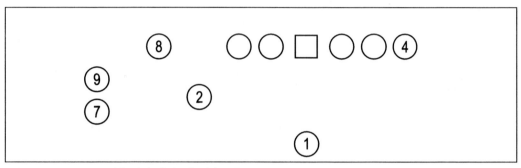

Diagram 2-4n. Double tight left, double wing

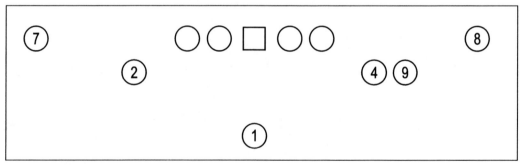

Diagram 2-4o. Formation 8: Pro right open, slot stack, backside tight

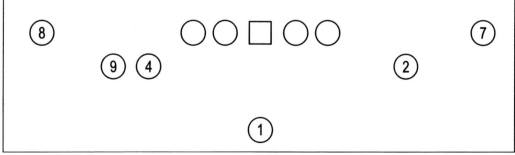

Diagram 2-4p. Pro left open, slot stack, backside tight

Game-Goals for the Empty Backfield

- Have no fumbles

- Rush for at least 120 yards per game

- Execute all "automatics"

- Properly block all blitzes

- Have no interceptions

- Complete at least 70% of passes

- Pass for at least 375 yards

- Catch all passes that hit the receiver's hands

- Have no bad "shotgun" snaps

- Attain positive yards on 75% of screens and draws

3

Offensive Line Run-Blocking Rules and Drills

The foundation of offensive football is in the play of the line, i.e. both tackles, both guards, the center, and sometimes the tight end. Their run blocking makes possible the running game, and their pass protection blocking enables the quarterback to pass the ball. The offensive line has the capability of shortening the game for an opponent, and lengthening the game for their own team.

Line Personnel

In order to perform well, offensive linemen need size, experience, strength, and quickness. It is more advantageous to be experienced rather than physically talented and better to be larger and stronger than smaller and faster. At these interior positions, a greater need exists for quickness than for foot speed. Special attention should be paid to strengthening the wrists, arms, shoulders, hips, and legs because these body parts come into play in everything the offensive lineman does. He must spend quality time in the weight room to develop strength in these areas.

With the advent of multiple odd and even defensive fronts and defensive stunts with linemen and linebackers, the offensive linemen have a great number of blocking adjustments to remember, while maintaining their composure when defenses change at the last minute. These skills and adjustments require ample time to learn and execute proper techniques. Current rules that allow the offensive linemen greater use of their hands have "leveled the playing field" for them. The rules have also placed a greater emphasis on the need for great strength, and increased emphasis on passing magnifies the need for bulk, as well as strength, in pass protection.

Base Blocking (One-on-One)

The spacing between the guard and center should be one-and-a-half yards; the tackles should be one to two yards away from the guards; and the tight ends should be one to two yards from the tackles. The purpose of this alignment is to split and isolate the defenders and thus give up the blocking angle to the offensive lineman.

Base Blocking Rule: Block the man over you. If no man over you, block first man to your inside. If no man inside on the line-of-scrimmage, block the linebacker.

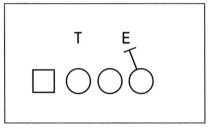

Diagram 3-1a.

Note: The defensive end is isolated from the defensive tackle, so the tight end has the blocking angle.

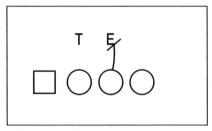

Diagram 3-1b.

Note: The defensive end refuses to be isolated, so he can be blocked by the offensive tackle.

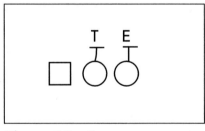

Diagram 3-2a. Over

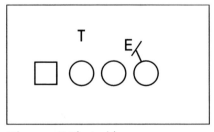

Diagram 3-2b. Inside

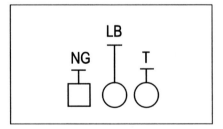

Diagram 3-2c. First linebacker

Stretch Run Blocking

With stretch blocking, the offensive linemen can either lead step or crossover step. If the lineman chooses to cross over, he steps at the middle of the defender with the off foot, anchor under the defender's armpit with the lead hand, anchor or step with the other foot while sticking the defender with the other hand, and maintain contact and block him wherever he wants to go.

Cross Blocking Rules

At the 0 Hole: (Diagram 3-3)

Center: block the first down lineman away from the hole

Left Guard: step around the center, block first down lineman past the center

Right Guard: drop step and block out on the tackle

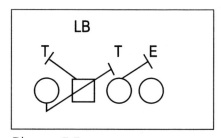

Diagram 3-3

At the 4 Hole: (Diagrams 3-4a and 3-4b)

Center: block the man over you, or the first man off the line of scrimmage.

Right Guard: if not covered, block out on the man over the tackle; if covered, step around the tackle and block the man over the tackle.

Right Tackle: block down on the man over the guard; if no man over the guard, step around the guard and block the first man off the line of scrimmage.

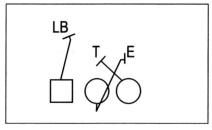

Diagram 3-4a. Even front

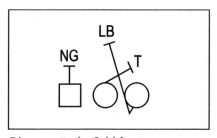

Diagram 3-4b. Odd front

At the 6 Hole: (Diagrams 3-5a and 3-5b)

Center: block the first man over or off the line of scrimmage.

Right Guard: block the man over or inside, or off the line of scrimmage.

Right Tackle: step around the tight end and block the first man over or outside the tight end.

Tight End or Slot Back: block down on the man over the tackle; if no man is over the tackle, block the first block down on the first linebacker to the inside.

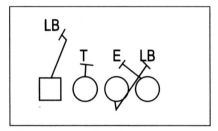

Diagram 3-5a. Even front

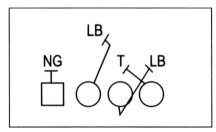

Diagram 3-5b. Odd front

At the 8 Hole: (Diagrams 3-6a and 3-6b)

Center: cut block the first man to the hole side.

Right Guard: "nick" the man over and scrape on the linebacker; if no man over, pull and lead to the hole.

Right Tackle: block the man over or inside on the linebacker.

Tight End or Slot Back: block the man over; if no man over, block the first linebacker.

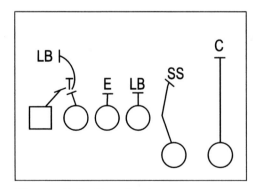

Diagram 3-6a. Even front

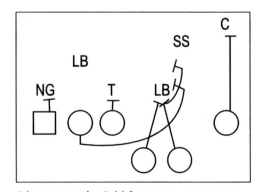

Diagram 3-6b. Odd front

Trap Blocking

At the 0 Hole: (Same rule as cross blocking)

At the 4 Hole: (Diagrams 3-7a and 3-7b)

Left Guard: Pull and trap the first man on the line of scrimmage past the right guard

Center: block man over or the first down lineman away from the hole

Right Guard: block man over or combo with the center to the backside linebacker

Right Tackle: Step behind the tight end and block the end man on the line of scrimmage

Tight End: block the near inside linebacker

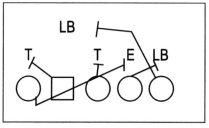

Diagram 3-7a. Even front

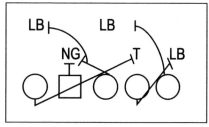

Diagram 3-7b. Odd front

At the 6 Hole: (Diagrams 3-8a through 3-8d)

Left Guard: Pull and trap the man on the end of the line of scrimmage.

Center: block the man over; if no man over, block down the lineman away from the hole.

Right Guard: block the man over; if no man over, combo with the center to the backside linebacker.

Right Tackle: block the man over.

Tight End or Slot: combo with the tackle to the inside linebacker.

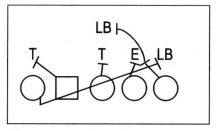

Diagram 3-8a. Even front

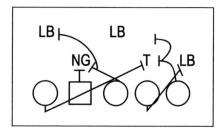

Diagram 3-8b. Odd front

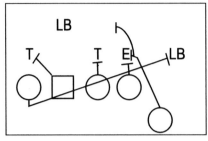

Diagram 3-8c. Even front

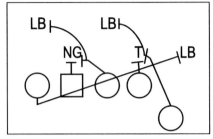

Diagram 3-8d. Odd front

Offensive Line Run-Blocking Drills (Diagrams 3-9a through 3-9e)

"Under the Chute"

Points of Emphasis:

- Stance and movement from the stance
- Hit on second step
- Lift and snap the head and hands up into the defender, walk legs up, lock elbows
- Drive the defender

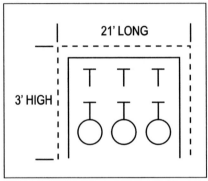

Diagram 3-9a.

Post Lead-Slip

Points of Emphasis:

Post Man (Diagram 3-9b)

- Step into the block with your inside foot (if defender disappears, continue on to the next level)
- Put the head and hands down the middle of the defender
- Throw your butt toward the lead man
- Lock out and drive the defender in a lateral direction

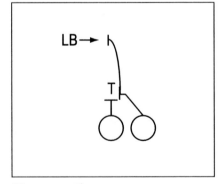

Diagram 3-9b.

Note: First concentrate on double-team block only—later double-team slip.

Lead Man

- Step into the defender with your inside foot (if the defender disappears, go to the next level)

- Drive the defender down the line for three steps, release and go to the next level and block the linebacker

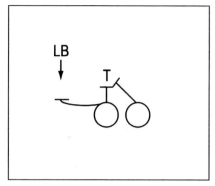

Diagram 3-9c.

Points of Emphasis:

- Lead step and snap your head and shoulders in the direction of the pull

- Stay close to the line of scrimmage and stay under control

- Emphasize blocking accuracy, later emphasize delivering a hard block

- Once the contact is made, work the defender into your own backfield; if the defender does not show, hook him at the line of scrimmage

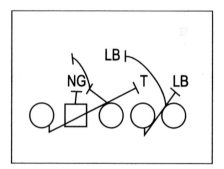

Diagram 3-9d.

Points of Emphasis:

- Guard will pull and lead to the point of attack

- Lock on the defender and drive him

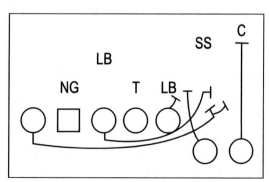

Diagram 3-9e.

4

Pass Protection

Good pass protection is essential to a successful passing attack. Quarterback sacks make getting first downs more difficult, unexpected hits to the quarterback can cause fumble-turnovers, and interceptions resulting from quarterback hurries can be demoralizing to the entire team. When a quarterback experiences good pass protection, he becomes more efficient, more confident, and more productive. With good protection, young quarterbacks with average arm strength can become highly effective. Interceptions and poorly thrown balls often are the result of faulty pass protection. A logical teaching progression dictates that pass protection should start with simple pass blocking techniques, and then systematically progress to more complex techniques and schemes such as protection against blitzing, stunts, and a variety of overloads. The quarterback must be involved in all protection schemes because his actions are based on the type of protection.

Pass protection for the empty backfield will be enhanced by the following:

- Using a "hot" receiver to take advantage of a blitzer to one side of the formation.

- Audibilizing to take advantage of a "mismatched" defender, i.e. a linebacker covering a wide receiver.

- Teaching the quarterback to pre-read coverages, read coverage after the snap, and release the ball between 1.9 seconds and 2.5 seconds.

- Audibilizing to adjust the pass protection versus blitz.

General Pass Protection Guidelines

On each pass play, the quarterback and other offensive players should count the number of possible defenders on their side of the center. This count should include linebackers and defensive backs, especially if the defensive back is in or near the "box," i.e. close to the line of scrimmage and between the tight ends.

Pass Blocking Drills
Guards and Center Blitz Pickup

Points of Emphasis:

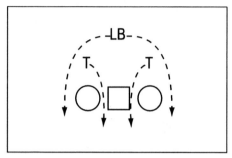

- Offensive line will drop as deep as possible to see the stunt, set with toes out and body angles closed, back arched, hands pressed to punch

- Talk to each other, pick up the proper blitzer and lock onto him

Diagram 4-1a.

Tackle, Tight End, and Wing Blitz Pickup

Points of Emphasis:

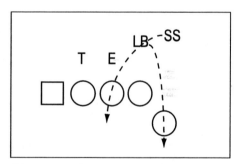

- Tight end and 4-back will drop deep to see the blitzers; set with toes pointed outward, body angles closed, back arched, hands ready to punch

- Talk to each other, pick up proper blitzer, and lock onto him

Diagram 4-1b.

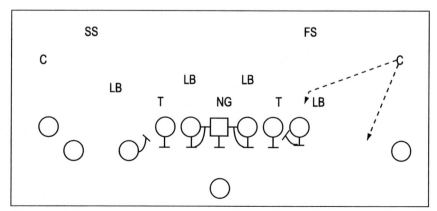

Diagram 4-1c.

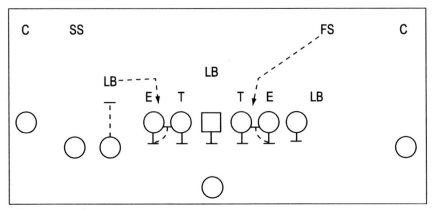

Diagram 4-1d.

The entire offense should be especially aware of fronts in which it may be outnumbered. (Diagrams 4-2a through 4-2h)

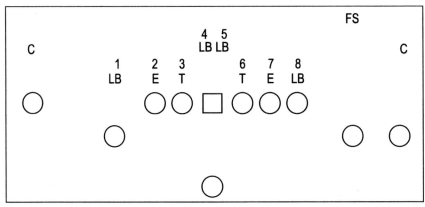

Diagram 4-2a. 4-4-3

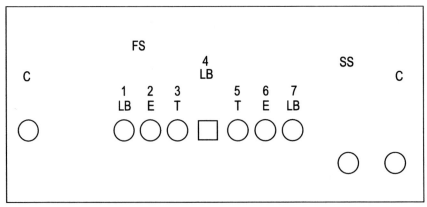

Diagram 4-2b. 4-3-4

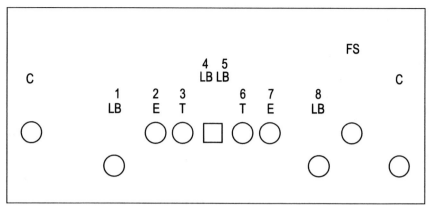

Diagram 4-2c. 4-4-3

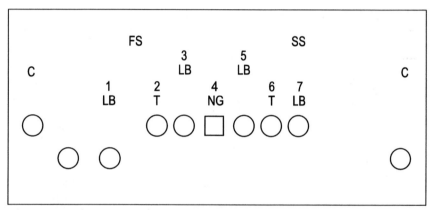

Diagram 4-2d. 3-4-4

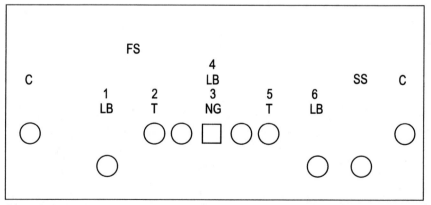

Diagram 4-2e. 3-3-5

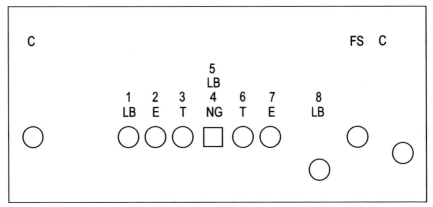

Diagram 4-2f. 5-3-3

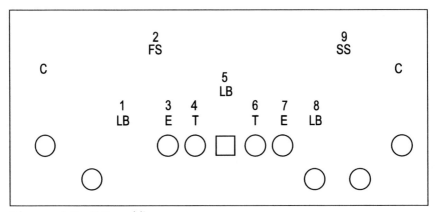

Diagram 4-2g. 6-5 goal line

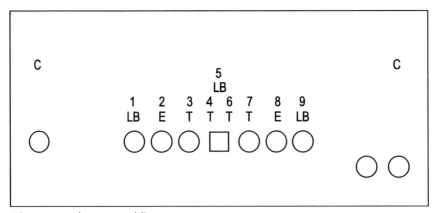

Diagram 4-2h. 8-3 goal line

The offensive line will adjust their pass blocking techniques based on the type of pass play and the defensive players' pass rush technique.

- On three-step drops with the quarterback under the center, the linemen will take on blockers with a line of scrimmage set, instead of drop stepping and setting up deep.

- On crossing stunts by defensive players, the offensive linemen must drop deeper in order to clearly see and react to the defenders' movements.

- On play-action passes, the linemen will "fire out" on defenders with the same initial move as if the play was a run, then drop and execute a regular pass block.

- If the defender steadily pushes the blocker back into the pocket, the blocker must disengage, drop lower, and stand his ground.

- The pass blocker should always keep his butt between the defender and the passer.

When the quarterback pre-reads a blitz, he can audible and signal to "hot" the blitz side of the offense or the vacated spot of the safety. The other side will block solid. (Diagram 4-3)

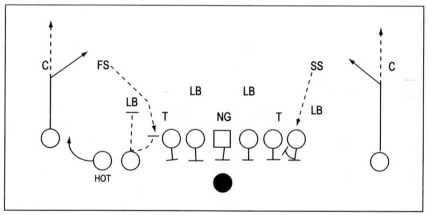

Diagram 4-3. If FS disappears run post; if not, fly. If SS disappears run post; if not, fly.

When the quarterback pre-reads inside stacking blitzers, he can signal the motion-man to block the closest blitzer to the center. This additional blocker can be called into play on any formation, and any situation. (Diagram 4-4)

The quarterback has the option of calling "solid" on any pass play. However, the quarterback must be taught that he can expect quick pressure from the outside with

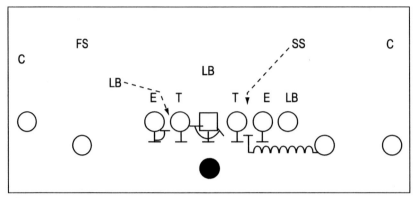

Diagram 4-4.

"solid" protection. Consequently, he must deliver the ball quickly on this call. Also, receivers must know that their routes must be cut shorter.

Solid protection will involve all interior linemen, the tight end, and slot or wing personnel. All players will zone block the gap to their inside, thereby creating a solid wall in front of the quarterback. (Diagrams 4-5a and 4-5b)

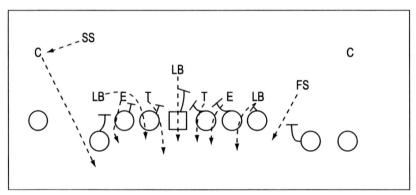

Diagram 4-5a. Even front

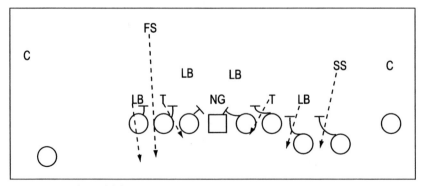

Diagram 4-5b. Odd front

Versus even fronts when the middle linebacker doesn't blitz, the center should look for a blitzing outside linebacker. The quarterback should be alert to slide away from the blitz side if pressured. The quarterback can also audibilize or signal a "hot" route by a receiver. (Diagrams 4-6a and 4-6b)

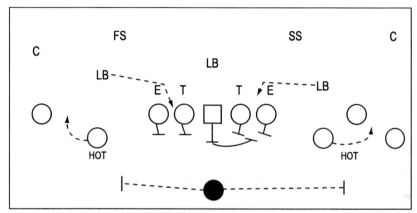

Diagram 4-6a. Slide to the right or left

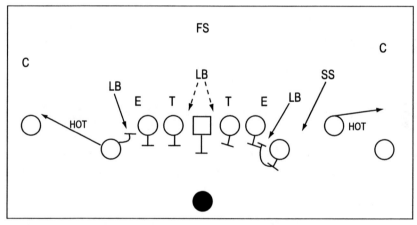

Diagram 4-6b. Overloaded blitz

5

The Empty Backfield Running Game

The running game in the empty backfield offense is a very important element in the overall offensive scheme. The 2-back, the 4-back, and the quarterback can all align in the shotgun position at various times. Of course, the quarterback can align under the center, depending on the type of running play desired.

Straight-ahead run plays, reverse plays, draw plays, bootleg plays, and option plays all add diversity to the running attack. This diversity prevents the defense from "stacking" their alignment to stop the pass. And if the defense assumes alignments aimed at stopping the pass, it becomes weaker against the run.

Teen Series

The Teen Series involves the player aligned under the center or in the shotgun position as the runner. Either the 2-back, 4-back, or quarterback will align in these positions, receive the snap from the center, and run the play called. (Diagrams 5-1a through 5-1l)

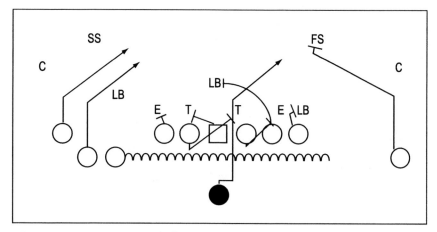

Diagram 5-1a. 10 Trap (O-hole trap blocking)

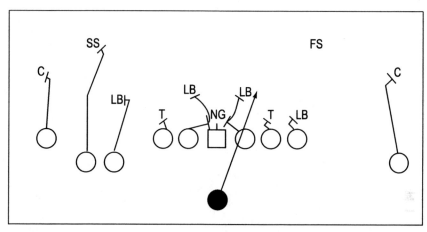

Diagram 5-1b. 10 (0-hole base blocking vs. odd)

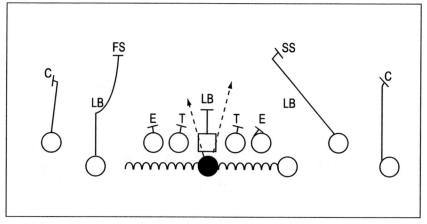

Diagram 5-1c. 10 (Quarterback sneak vs. even)

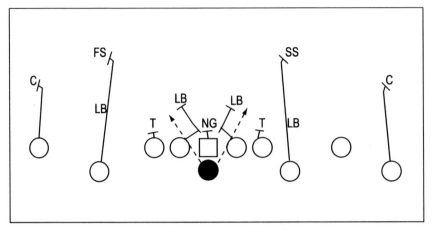

Diagram 5-1d. 10 (Quarterback sneak vs. odd)

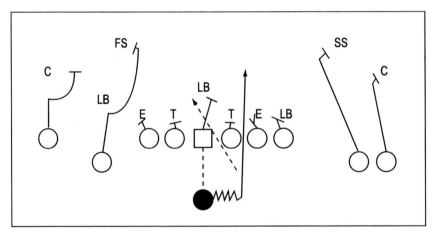

Diagram 5-1e. 14 (4-hole base blocking vs. even)

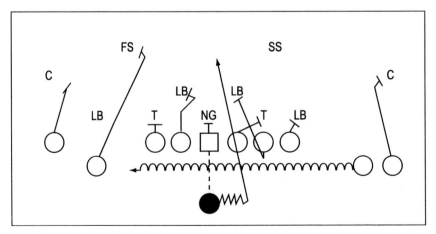

Diagram 5-1f. 14 (4-hole cross blocking vs. odd)

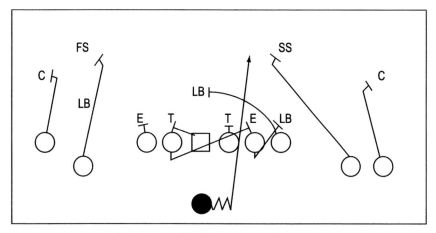

Diagram 5-1g. 14 (4-hole trap blocking vs. even)

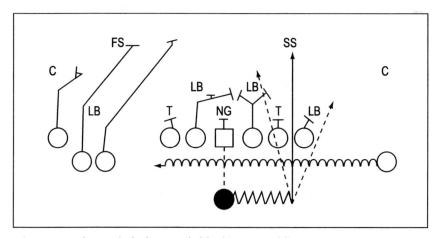

Diagram 5-1h. 16 (6-hole stretch blocking vs. odd)

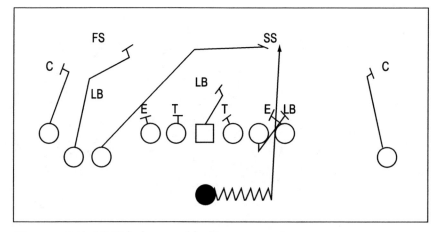

Diagram 5-1i. 16 (6-hole cross blocking vs. even)

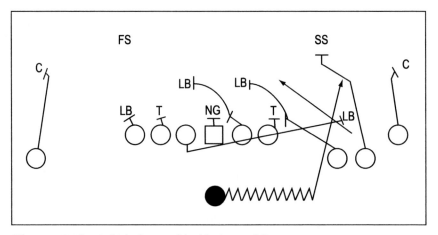

Diagram 5-1j. 16 (6-hole trap blocking vs. odd)

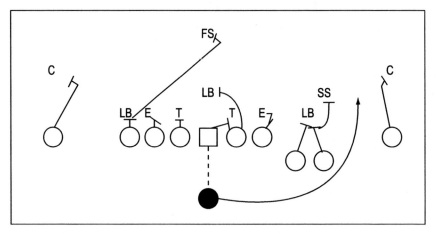

Diagram 5-1k. 18 (8-hole cross blocking vs. even)

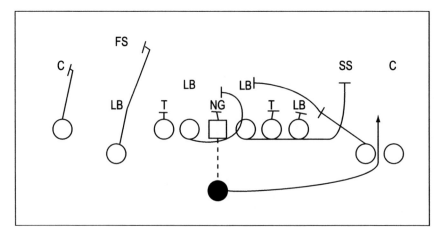

Diagram 5-1l. 18 (8-hole cross blocking vs. odd)

The Option Series (Diagrams 5-2a and 5-2b)

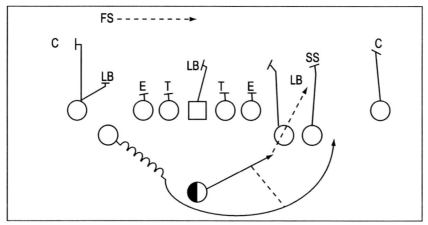

Diagram 5-2a. 28 motion, 18 option

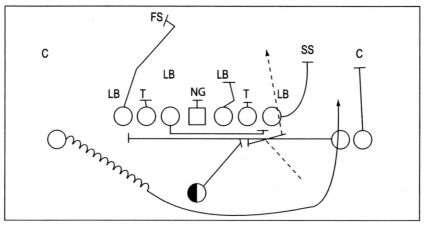

Diagram 5-2b. 25C, 18 option

The Sweep Series (diagrams 5-3a and 5-3b)

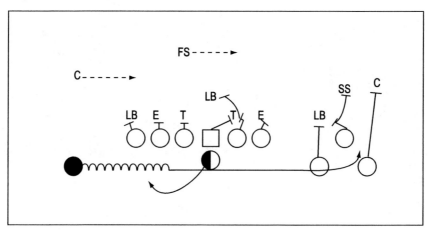

Diagram 5-3a. 98 flanker motion

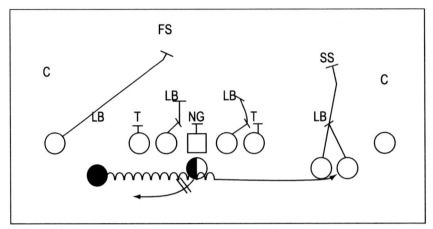

Diagram 5-3b. 28 slot motion

The Counter Series (Diagrams 5-4a through 5-4s)

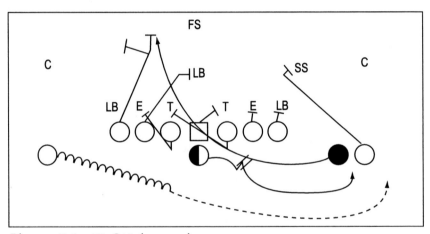

Diagram 5-4a. 16, C41 (vs. even)

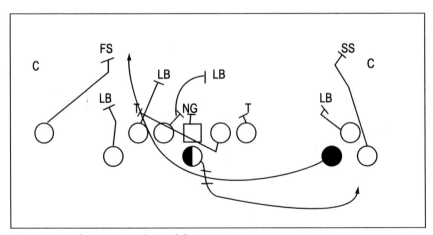

Diagram 5-4b. 16, C43 (vs. odd)

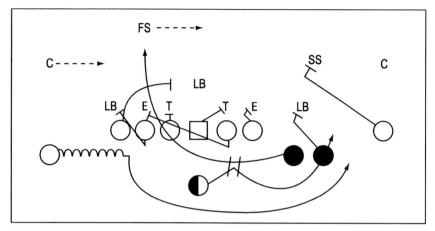

Diagram 5-4c. 16c C43 (quarterback in shotgun)

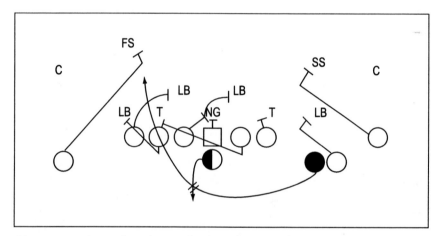

Diagram 5-4d. 16, C43 (quarterback under center)

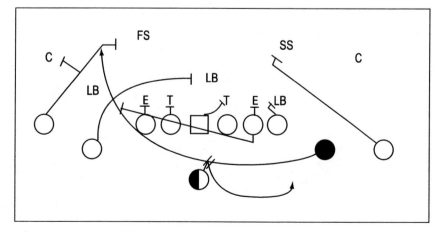

Diagram 5-4e. 16, C45

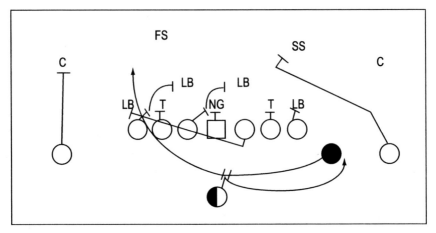

Diagram 5-4f. 16, C25

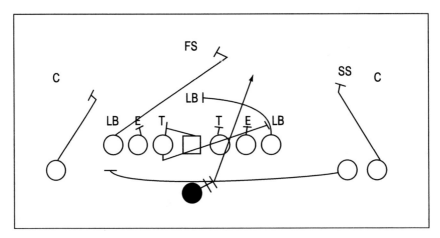

Diagram 5-4g. 25, C14

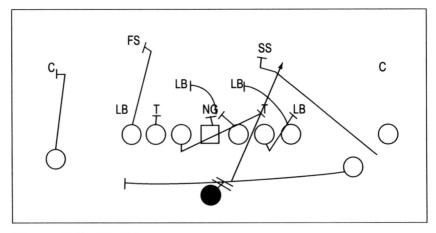

Diagram 5-4h. 25, C14

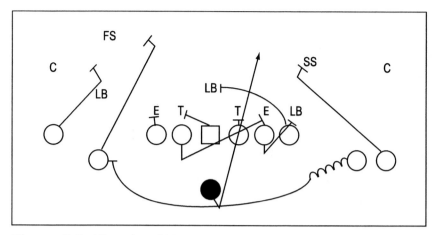

Diagram 5-4i. 45 motion, C14

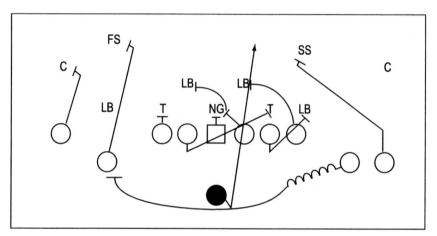

Diagram 5-4j. 45 motion, C14

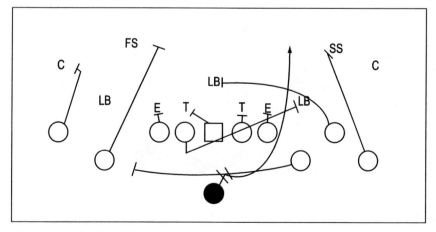

Diagram 5-4k. 45, C14

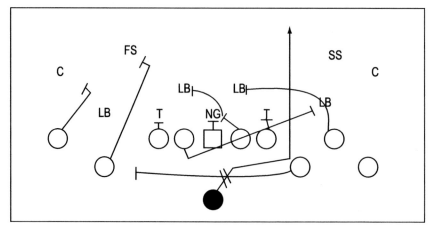

Diagram 5-4l. 45, C16

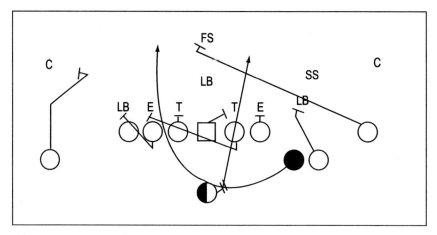

Diagram 5-4m. 14, C43

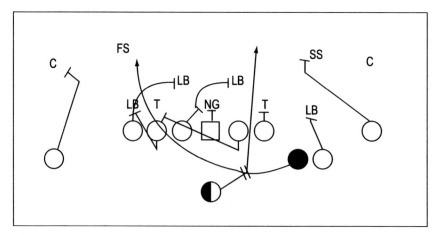

Diagram 5-4n. 14, C43

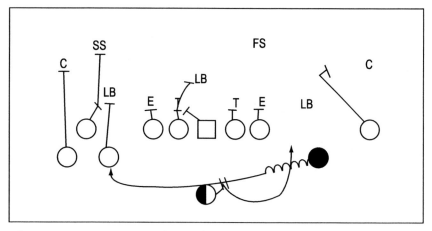

Diagram 5-4o. 16, C48 motion

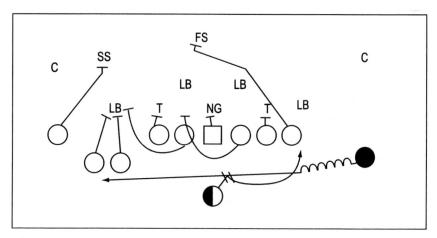

Diagram 5-4p. 16, C48 motion

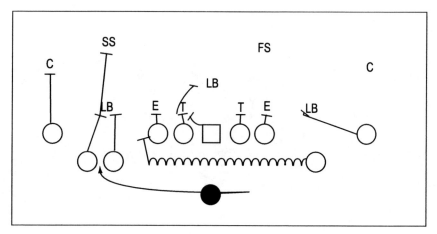

Diagram 5-4q. 18, C17, motion 27

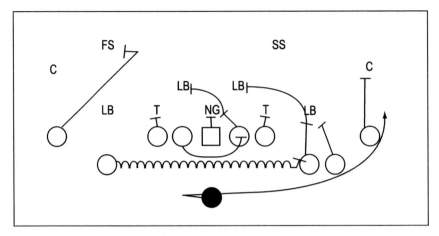

Diagram 5-4r. 17, C18, motion 28

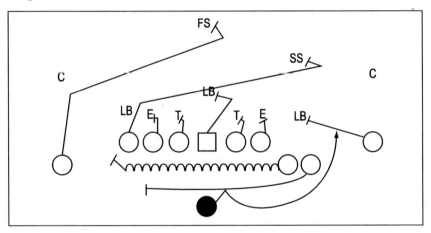

Diagram 5-4s. 45, C18

Reverses (Diagrams 5-5a through 5-5e)

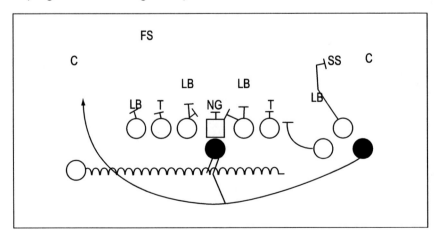

Diagram 5-5a. 78 motion, reverse

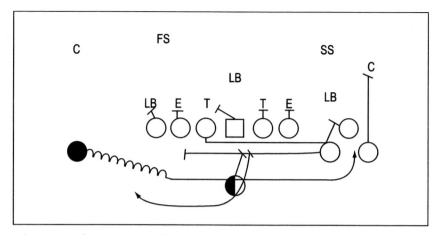

Diagram 5-5b. 16C, 45, split end reverse

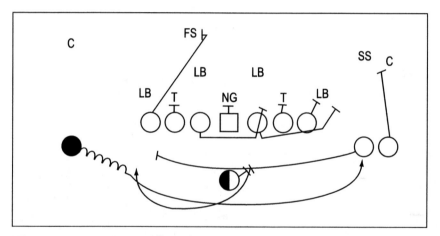

Diagram 5-5c. 16C, 25, split end reverse

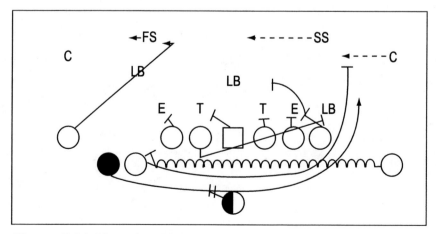

Diagram 5-5d. 98 motion, 28 reverse

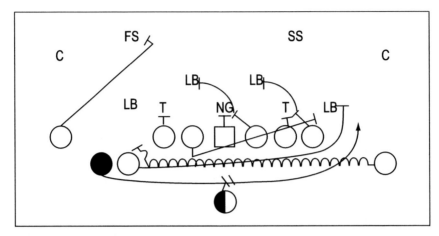

Diagram 5-5e. 98 motion, 28 reverse

Skill Development for the Running Game

Simplicity is the key to developing efficient skills for the empty backfield running game. Time constraints are the primary reason for the need of simplicity, because the majority of practice time in the empty backfield offense should be spent practicing the passing game.

Blocking by the Receivers

The slot and wide receivers are taught three basic blocks:

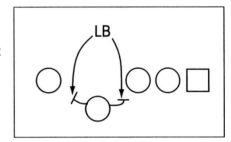

Diagram 5-6. Backside cut-off block by the slot

- Backside cut-off block

- Stalk block

- Cut block (high school rules may prohibit blocking below the waist)

   The backside cut-off block is used primarily by the slot receiver on run plays away from his side. (Diagram 5-6)

Points of Emphasis:

- Take a short jab step with the inside foot and stay on balance.

- Wait until the defender commits in one direction or the other.

- When the defender commits, the back will then block him away from the run side.

The stalk block is the most frequently used block to the run side of the play. (Diagrams 5-7a and 5-7b)

Points of Emphasis:

- Drive hard off the line of scrimmage until you are three to four yards away from the defender.

- Break down and come under control; widen your feet; position your body between the defender and the point of attack; extend the arms and attack the defender with your hands on his jersey numbers.

- Keep contact with the defender and push him wherever he wants to go.

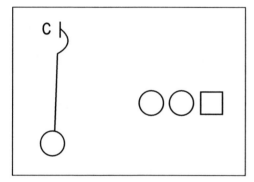

Diagram 5-7a. Stalk block

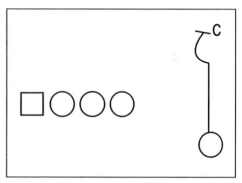

Diagram 5-7b.

The cut block is used both to the playside and the backside of running plays. As was noted previously, high school rules may prohibit blocking below the waist, thus this block should only be taught at the college level. (Diagram 5-8)

Points of Emphasis:

- Drive hard off the line of scrimmage until you are within arm's distance from the defender.

- Extend your arm and shoulder past the defender's thigh.

- If the blocker is able to stay on his feet, roll into his legs.

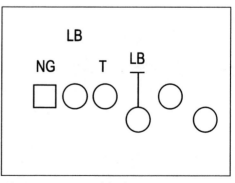

Diagram 5-8. Cut block

Blocking by the Tight End

The tight end in the empty backfield offense needs to learn both the receiver's blocking skills when he is split away from the tackle, and offensive line blocking skills when aligned close to the tackle. Because the tight end is required to do more blocking than the other receivers, he should spend more time developing these skills, particularly with the offensive line.

Faking by the Quarterback, the Slot, and Receivers

Good faking is critically important to the success of the counter, the draw, and reverse run plays. The quarterback and receivers should be convincing ballcarrier fakers. As fake ballcarriers, they need to influence the defenders to react to the "decoy," rather than to the actual ballcarrier. The quarterback and receivers should follow the same procedures when faking as when actually receiving a handoff or toss and running with the ball.

Receiving the Handoff

A properly received handoff is the responsibility of both the quarterback and the ballcarrier. The quarterback's responsibility is to securely place the ball in the ballcarrier's "pocket," and then to carry out a convincing fake. Once the ball has been placed in the ballcarrier's pocket, it is his responsibility to "lock it up" and never fumble.

Points of emphasis for the ballcarrier during and after the handoff include:

- Bend at the waist; keep your head up and eyes focused on the run hole.
- The ballside elbow is up, the palm is down, and the fingers are spread.
- The bottom side palm is up, and the fingers are spread.
- Close the fingers over the far end of the ball.
- Once in the run hole, run toward the goal line. Try to avoid zigzag and stutter steps until past the line of scrimmage.
- Break tackles and score!

Ballcarrier Drills (Diagrams 5-9a through 5-9e)

Points of Emphasis:

- Proper handoff mechanics.

- Forward body lean with balance when running between the two air bags.

- Quick foot action when running over the two cylinder bags.

- Lift with the forearm and shoulder when contacted by the last three air bags.

- Finish by sprinting past the goal line.

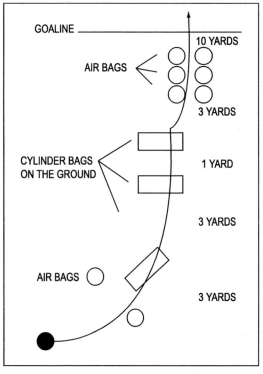

Diagram 5-9a. Sideline running drill

Points of Emphasis:

- Proper handoff mechanics.

- Forward body lean with balance when running through the two air bags.

- Quick foot action when running over the cylinder bag.

- Finish by sprinting past the goal line.

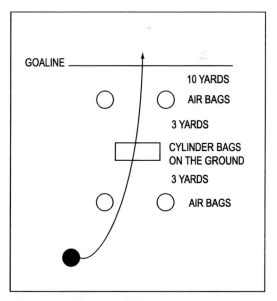

Diagram 5-9b. Dive drill

Points of Emphasis:

- Proper handoff mechanics.

- Eyes focused on goal line, motion the bags.

- Quick foot action when running over the cylinder bags.

- First repetition—single foot between bags. Second repetition—two feet between bags.

- Finish by sprinting past the goal line.

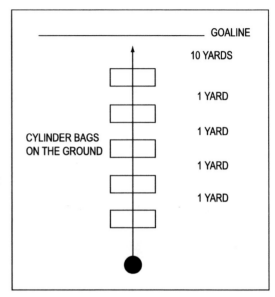

Diagram 5-9c. High knee drill

Points of Emphasis:

- Proper handoff mechanics.

- Forward body lean with balance when running between the first two air bags.

- Quick foot action when running over the cylinder bags.

- Maintain agility and balance when spinning off the standup cylinder bags.

- Lift with the forearm and shoulder when contacted by the last two air bags.

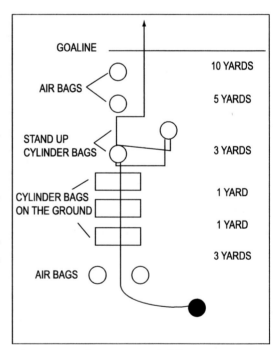

Diagram 5-9d. Burma road drill

Points of Emphasis:

- Proper handoff mechanics.

- Forward body lean with balance when running between the first two air bags.

- Quick foot action when running over the cylinder bags.

- Keep shoulders square and low when running between the last four air bags.

- Finish by sprinting past the goal line.

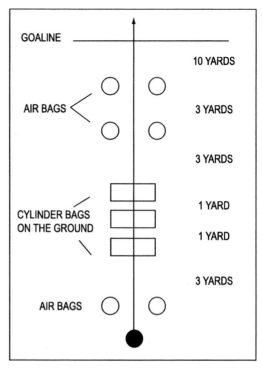

Diagram 5-9e. Bread and butter drill

Play Timing Drills (Diagrams 5-10a through 5-10f)

All ballcarrier personnel and the quarterback will be used in the play timing drill. All running plays in the empty backfield offense can be practiced in this drill.

Note: Use a line spacer to establish all of the holes from end to end, and therefore provide accurate spacing for play timing. Handheld air bags can also be used to emphasize running hard past the line of scrimmage.

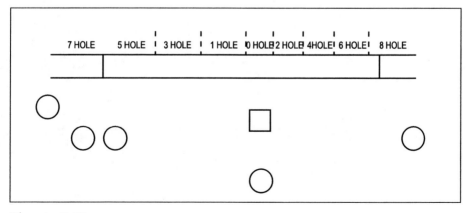

Diagram 5-10a.

Note: Run to both sides

Points of Emphasis:

- Proper handoff mechanics.
- Quarterback carry out the fake.
- Running back squares his shoulders as he runs through the line of scrimmage.
- Finish by sprinting past the goal line.

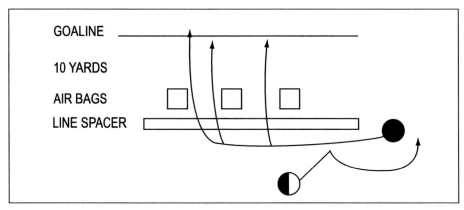

Diagram 5-10b. Counter play timing

Note: Run to both sides

Points of Emphasis:

- Proper handoff fake, and counter fake by the back.
- The quarterback squares his shoulders as he runs through the line of scrimmage.
- Finish by sprinting past the goal line.

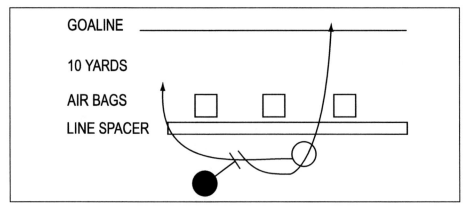

Diagram 5-10c. Fake counter, stretch play timing

Note: Run to both sides

Points of Emphasis:

- Proper handoff fake and counter fake by the back.

- The quarterback will run at the inside hip of the outside linebacker. Pitch if he takes the quarterback; keep if he takes the pitch man.

- Finish by sprinting past the goal line.

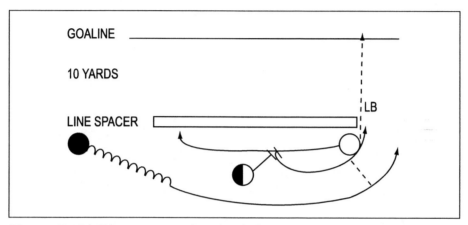

Diagram 5-10d. Fake counter, option play timing

Note: Run to both sides

Points of Emphasis:

- Proper handoff fake and counter fake by the back.

- Quarterback reverse spin and handoff to the reverse back, then carry out bootleg fake.

- Finish by sprinting past the goal line.

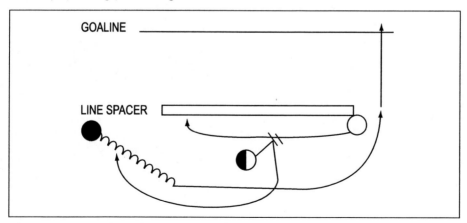

Diagram 5-10e. Fake counter, reverse play timing

Note: Run to both sides

Points of Emphasis:

- The quarterback reads the outside linebacker.
- If the linebacker takes the quarterback, he shovel passes to the back.
- If the linebacker takes the shovel back, the quarterback keeps the ball and runs outside.
- Finish by sprinting past the goal line.

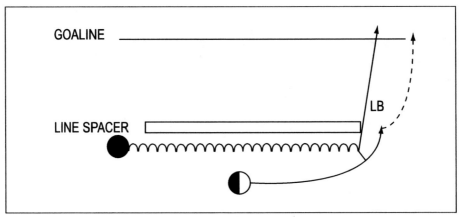

Diagram 5-10f. Shovel pass play timing

6

Developing the Empty Backfield Passing Game

It is in the passing game that the empty backfield offense takes on a "life of its own." As was emphasized in Chapter 1, the awareness and handling of the blitz is of utmost importance to the success of the empty backfield passing game.

Pass protection (Chapter 4) is essential to a successful passing attack. Offensive linemen must be able to block blitzing linebackers and defensive line stunts. The tight end and slot receivers must be prepared to block blitzing outside linebackers or defensive backs.

The quarterback is also responsible for his own protection. He must always pre-read where all the linebackers are located, as well as any defensive back in a blitzing position. If the quarterback pre-reads the blitz, he can either signal for a receiver to run a "hot" route, or audibilize to a pattern "hot" or "blitz beater" route. If the defense disguises the blitz until after a snap, the quarterback must make a quick post-snap adjustment and throw to his pre-determined "hot" receiver before being sacked.

The Quarterback Read System

After the snap in the read system, the quarterback is required to look at one or two defenders to determine what they are doing, and then to select a receiver based on what he sees. The quarterback is also required to be aware of what is happening in the vicinity of his read. This is called "feel." (Example: double-teaming a receiver). The coach should also teach the quarterback to find an isolated or one-on-one situation on a receiver, and take advantage of his man coverage by throwing to the isolated receiver.

The technique of "read" and "feel" will require the coach to teach the quarterback to widen his peripheral vision. The coach can also help his quarterback by designing pass patterns that are applicable to both man and zone coverages—i.e., patterns that either horizontally or vertically stretch the secondary zones. (Diagram 6-1)

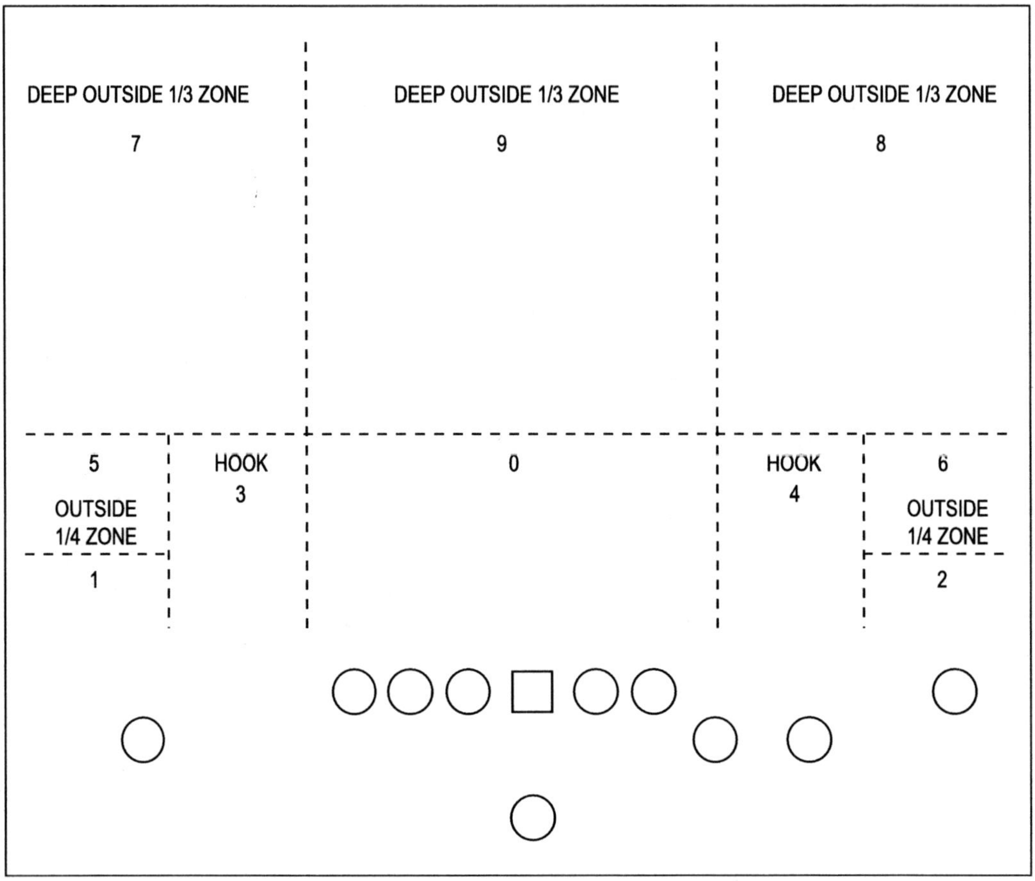

Diagram 6-1

Note: The three deep zones can be stretched to the back of the end zone. The outside quarter zones can be stretched to the sideline. And the hook zones and the middle zone can be stretched from the line of scrimmage to a point deep into the secondary.

This is done by placing two receivers in a zone and forcing the defense to either cover one or the other; or bring a defender from another zone to help cover a receiver. In either situation, the offense creates problems for the defense.

Half-Field Passing Drills

The following are examples of half-field drills that can be designed to teach the quarterback the "read and feel" system. Of course, the route combinations are almost limitless, thus the coach must select those patterns that can be taught easily and have a chance to be successful versus both man and zone coverages. (Diagrams 6-2a through 6-2t)

Note: Run to both sides

Points of Emphasis:

- The quarterback reads the outside linebacker and safety.

- If the outside linebacker blitzes, throw "hot."

- If the outside linebacker covers the outside quarter, throw to the split end on either a post or fly.

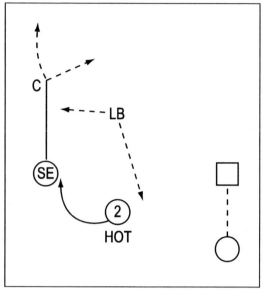

Diagram 6-2a

Note: Run to both sides

Points of Emphasis:

- The quarterback and split end pre-read to find the safety.

- If no safety, the split end runs the post.

- If the safety is to his side, the split end runs the fly.

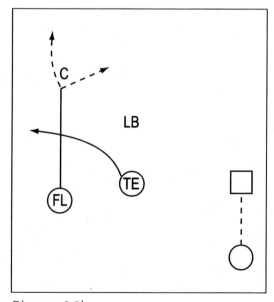

Diagram 6-2b

Note: Run to both sides

Points of Emphasis:

- The quarterback pre-reads to find the saftey.

- The quarterback makes good fakes.

- The quarterback reads the outside linebacker and cornerback, and throws to either the tightend or 2-back.

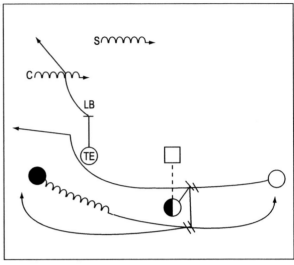

Diagram 6-2c

Note: Run to both sides

Points of Emphasis:

- The quarterback reads the outside linebacker.

- If the outside linebacker blitzes, throw "hot."

- If the outside linebacker drops, throw to the split end.

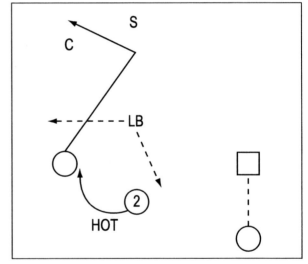

Diagram 6-2d

Note: Run to both sides

Points of Emphasis:

- The quarterback reads the outside linebacker and corner.

- If the outside linebacker blitzes, throw to the two back.

- If the outside linebacker drops, throw to the split end, or the two back if mismatched.

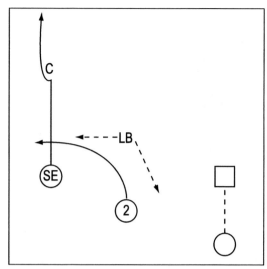

Diagram 6-2e

Note: Run to both sides

Points of Emphasis:

- The quarterback reads the corner.

- If the corner covers the deep third, throw to either the tight end or two back.

- If the corner covers the outside quarter, throw to the flanker.

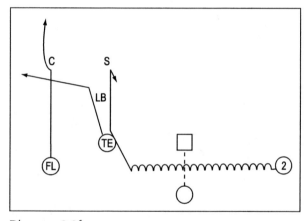

Diagram 6-2f

Note: Run to both sides

Points of Emphasis:

- The quarterback reads the corner and feels the safety.

- The quarterback will throw to either the tight end or the flanker.

- If the outside linebacker blitzes, throw to the two back.

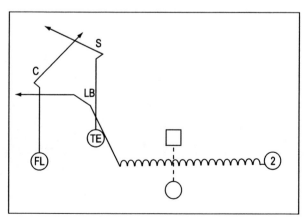

Diagram 6-2g

Note: Run to both sides

Points of Emphasis:

- The quarterback reads the corner and feels the safety.

- The quarterback will throw to either the 4-back or the split end, depending on what the corner does.

- If the safety covers the 4-back, throw to the tight end.

Note: The quarterback must carry the ball shoulder high with both hands to help turn his shoulders downfield.

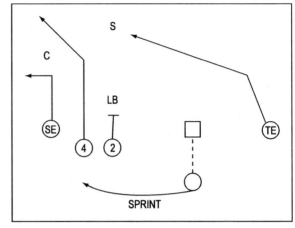

Diagram 6-2h

Note: Run to both sides

Points of Emphasis:

- The quarterback reads the outside linebacker.
- If the outside linebacker blitzes, throw to the 2-back.
- If the outside linebacker drops, throw to the split end.

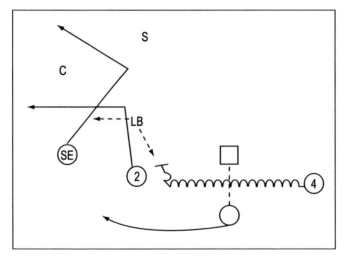

Diagram 6-2i

Note: Run to both sides

Points of Emphasis:

- The quarterback reads the safety and corner, and feels the outside linebacker.

- If the outside linebacker drops, throw to the 4-back or flanker.

- If the outside linebacker blitzes, throw to the tight end.

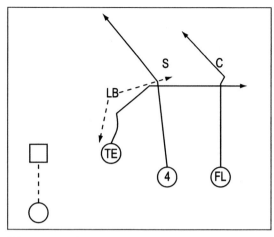

Diagram 6-2j

Note: Run to both sides

Points of Emphasis:

- The quarterback reads the corner and feels the safety.

- The quarterback will throw to either the flanker or the tight end.

- If the 4-back beats the safety deep, throw to him.

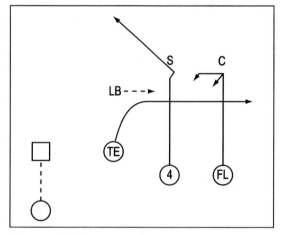

Diagram 6-2k

Note: Run to both sides

Points of Emphasis:

- The quarterback reads the corner and feels the safety.

- The quarterback will throw to either the flanker or the tight end.

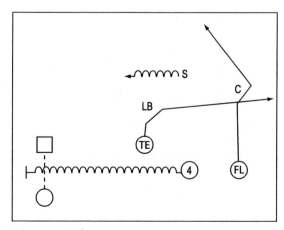

Diagram 6-2l

Note: Run to both sides

Points of Emphasis:

- The quarterback reads the corner and feels the safety.

- The quarterback will throw to either the flanker or the 4-back.

- The tight end will block to the linebacker if he blitzes.

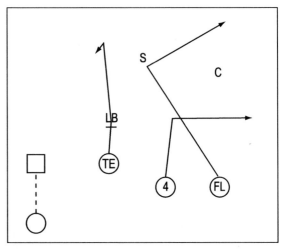

Diagram 6-2m

Note: Run to both sides

Points of Emphasis:

- The quarterback reads the corner and feels the safety.

- The quarterback will throw to either the flanker or the tight end.

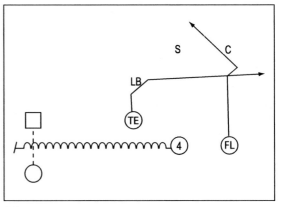

Diagram 6-2n

Note: Run to both sides

Points of Emphasis:

- The quarterback reads the linebackers to the tight end side.

- If the linebackers zone drop, throw to the tight end.

- If the outside linebacker blitzes, throw to the 4-back.

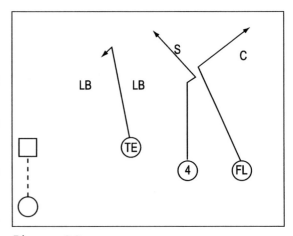

Diagram 6-2o

Note: Run to both sides

Points of Emphasis:

- The quarterback reads the corner and feels the safety.

- The quarterback throws to either the tight end or the flanker.

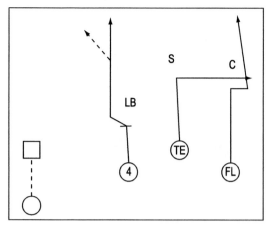

Diagram 6-2p

Note: Run to both sides

Points of Emphasis:

- The quarterback reads the corner and feels the safety.

- The quarterback will throw to either the 4-back or the flanker.

- The tight end will block the outside linebacker if he blitzes.

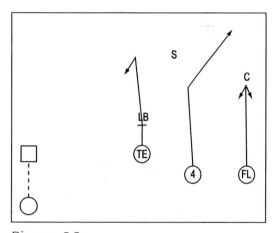

Diagram 6-2q

Note: Run to both sides

Points of Emphasis:

- The quarterback reads the linebackers to the tight end side and feels the safety.

- If the linebackers zone drop, throw to the tight end.

- If the safety covers the 4-back, throw to the flanker.

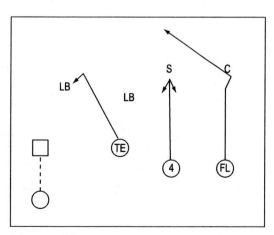

Diagram 6-2r

Note: Run to both sides

Points of Emphasis:

- The quarterback reads the outside linebacker and feels the corner.

- The quarterback will throw to either the 2-back or the 4-back.

- If the corner covers the outside quarter, throw to the split end.

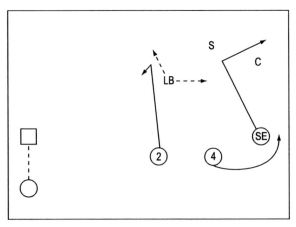

Diagram 6-2s

Note: Run to both sides

Points of Emphasis:

- The quarterback reads the corner and feels the safety.

- If the corner covers the outside quarter, throw to the flanker or tight end.

- If the corner covers the deep third, throw to the 2-back or the tight end.

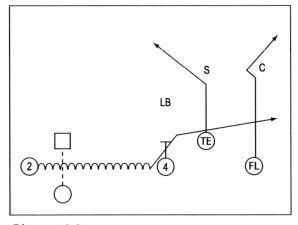

Diagram 6-2t

Pass Skeleton Drill

The next progression in the development of the empty backfield passing game is the pass skeleton drill. This drill involves the six pass eligible offensive players plus the center, and either six, seven, or eight defenders. The pass skeleton drill can be set up in a variety of field positions and/or down-and-distance situations to simulate conditions. The coach should emphasize that all players participate at full-speed, but not allow tackling.

If videotaping this drill is not feasible, the coach should assign a manager or another coach the responsibility of recording the following for each quarterback and receiver participating in the drill:

- Completions
- Balls thrown too late
- Poorly thrown passes
- Interceptions

- Catches
- Drops
- Missed assignment (wrong route by a receiver)
- Fumbles after the catch

The total of these situations over a period of time will help in the selection of the most efficient quarterback and receivers. These players should receive the majority of game playing time, and give the team the best chance for success.

The coach can also include "scramble" situations in the skeleton drill. The quarterback will execute his drop, but instead of throwing "on time," will roll-out either right or left to throw or run. The receivers are taught to adjust their routes toward the side of the quarterback's scramble, and find open areas. The quarterback should look for "open" receivers to the side of the scramble, but not be allowed to throw late to a receiver in the middle of the field. The quarterback should also be taught to run for the "first down," or throw out-of-bounds to avoid a sack and negative yardage.

An excellent and necessary team situation is the team "blitz" period (Diagram 6-3). All elements of the passing game versus blitzing defenses should be incorporated into this practice period, including:

- Pass protection
- Pre-snap reads
- Reads after the snap
- "Hot" route adjustments
- Audibles to "blitz beater" patterns

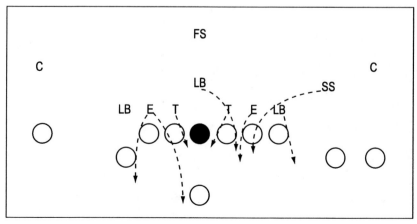

Diagram 6-3. Team blitz pickup

7

The Empty Backfield Passing Game

The next obvious progression in developing the empty backfield passing game is to incorporate the elements of pass protection and pass patterns into a team situation. The team situation can be full speed with live blocking, but no live tackling. Or, it can be a game-simulated scrimmage situation with line blocking, and line tackling of the receivers and runners. The coach should make the rules clear to all players in the scrimmage situation to avoid injury to an unaware player.

As has been previously emphasized, an unlimited number of pass protections and pass patterns exist. However, the coach should select a limited number of plays for each game that he believes can be easily learned and executed versus both man and zone coverages. Following are examples of drop back and sprint-out pass plays in the empty backfield offense.

Drop Back Pass Patterns

Double Tight, Wing Right (Diagrams 7-1 through 7-4)

Quarterback read:

- Strong safety throw to 2, 9, or 8
- Free safety throw to 4 or 7

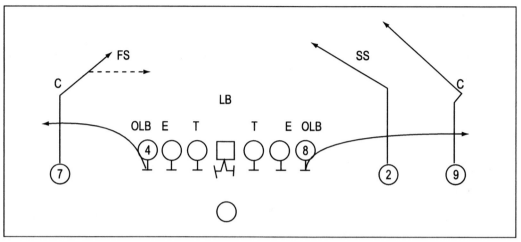

Diagram 7-1

Quarterback read:

- Strong safety throw to 2, 9, or 8
- Free safety throw to 4 or 7

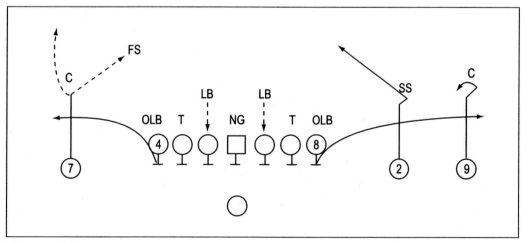

Diagram 7-2

Quarterback read:

- Left cornerback throw to 4 or 7
- Right cornerback throw to 8 or 9

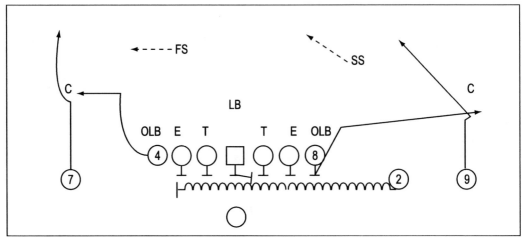

Diagram 7-3

Quarterback read:

- Right cornerback throw to 2, 9, or 8
- Left cornerback throw to 4 or 7

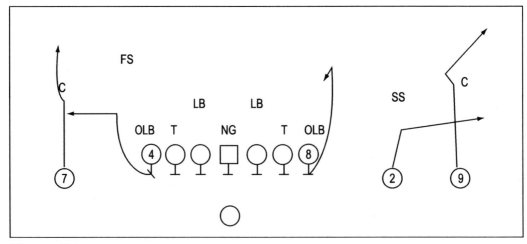

Diagram 7-4

Pro Right, Trips Right, Slot Left (Diagrams 7-5 through 7-10)

Quarterback read:

- Left outside linebacker throw to 2 or 7
- Right strong safety throw to 4 or 9

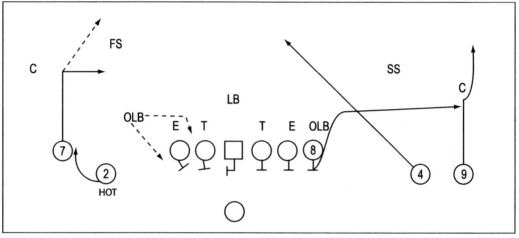

Diagram 7-5

Quarterback read:

- Left outside linebacker throw to 2 or 7
- Right outside linebacker throw to 8, 4, or 9

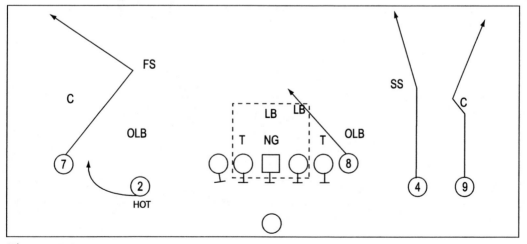

Diagram 7-6

Quarterback read:

- Left outside linebacker throw to 2 or 7
- Right cornerback throw to 4, 9, or 8

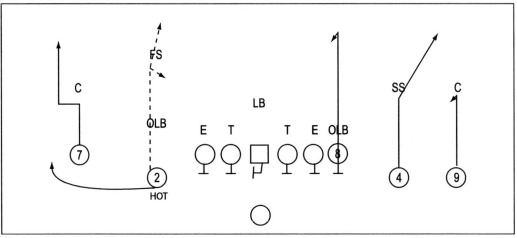

Diagram 7-7

Quarterback read:

- Left cornerback throw to 2 or 7
- Left strong safety/right strong safety throw to 9

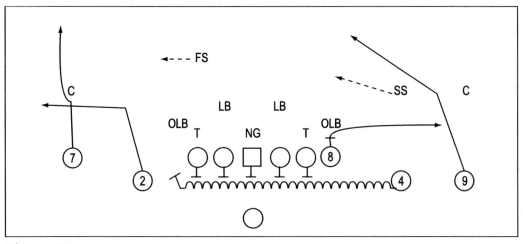

Diagram 7-8

Quarterback read:

- Left outside linebacker throw to 2 or 7
- Right outside linebacker throw to 4, 9, or 8

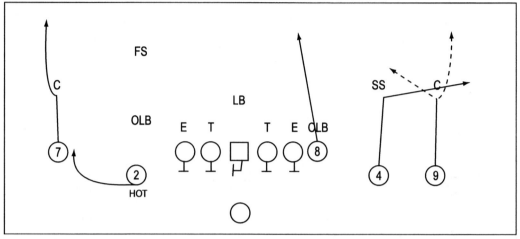

Diagram 7-9

Quarterback read:

- Left outside linebacker and left cornerback throw to 2 or 7
- Strong safety throw to 9 or 7

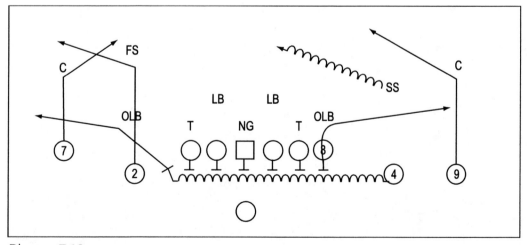

Diagram 7-10

Pro Right Open, Slot Left (Diagrams 7-11 through 7-15)

Quarterback read:

- Left outside linebacker throw to 2 or 7
- Strong safety throw to 4 or 9

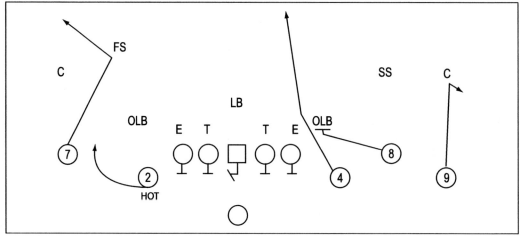

Diagram 7-11

Quarterback read:

- Left outside linebacker throw to 2 or 7
- Right cornerback throw to 8 or 9

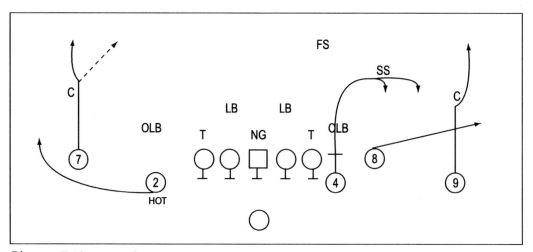

Diagram 7-12

Quarterback read:

- Right cornerback throw to 4, 9, or 8
- Left outside linebacker throw to 2 or 7

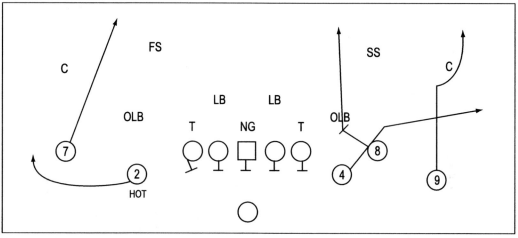

Diagram 7-13

Quarterback read:

- Right cornerback throw to 8, 9, or 4
- Left outside linebacker throw to 2 or 7

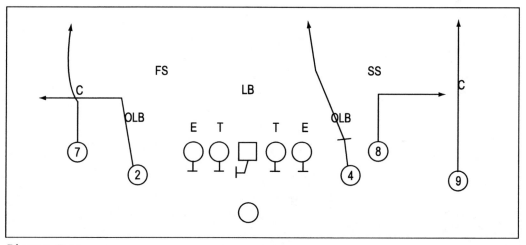

Diagram 7-14

Quarterback read:

- Right cornerback throw to 4 or 8

- Left outside linebacker throw to 2 or 7

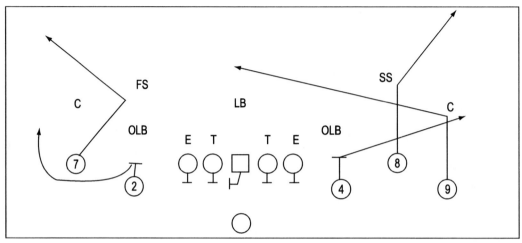

Diagram 7-15

Pro Left, Double Slot Right (Diagrams 7-16 through 7-19)

Quarterback read:

- Free safety/strong safety throw to 4, 2, or 7

- Left cornerback throw to 8 or 9

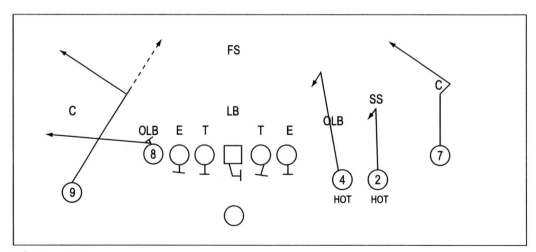

Diagram 7-16

Quarterback read:

- Left outside linebacker throw to 8 or 9
- Strong safety/cornerback throw to 2 or 7

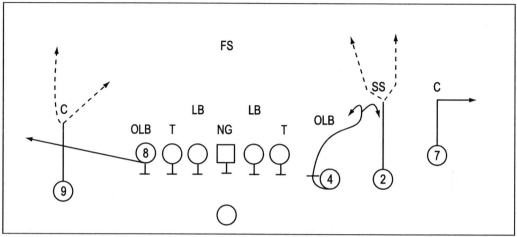

Diagram 7-17

Quarterback read:

- Right outside linebacker throw to 2, 4, or 7
- Left outside linebacker throw to 9 or 8

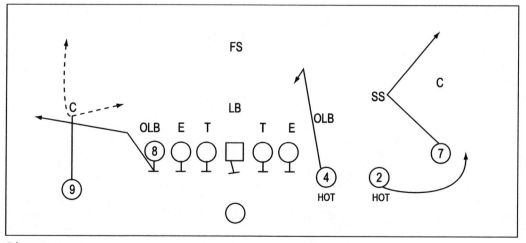

Diagram 7-18

Quarterback read:

- Free safety throw to 9, 8, or 7
- Right cornerback throw to 2

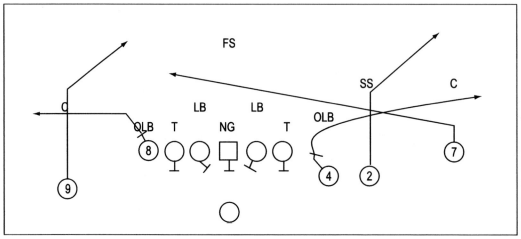

Diagram 7-19

Pro Right Open, Slot Stack, Backside Tight (Diagram 7-20)

Quarterback read:

- Strong safety/free safety throw to 8, 9, or 7
- Left cornerback throw to 4

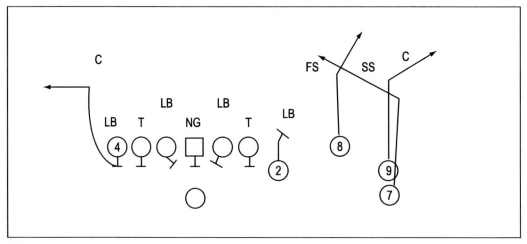

Diagram 7-20

Pro Right, Double Slot Left, Motion (Diagrams 7-21 and 7-22)

Quarterback read:

• Left cornerback throw to 7, 2, or 4

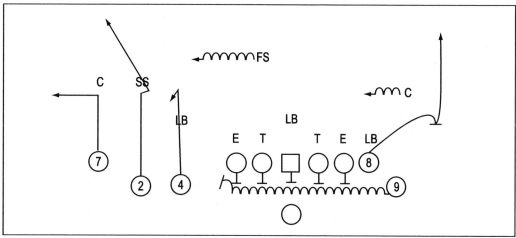

Diagram 7-21

Quarterback read:

• Strong safety throw to 7 or 2

• Left cornerback throw to 7 or 4

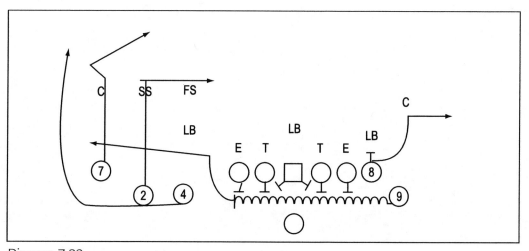

Diagram 7-22

Pro Right Open, Slot Right, Backside Tight (Diagram 7-23)

Quarterback read:

- Right cornerback throw to 7 or 9

- Free safety throw to 8

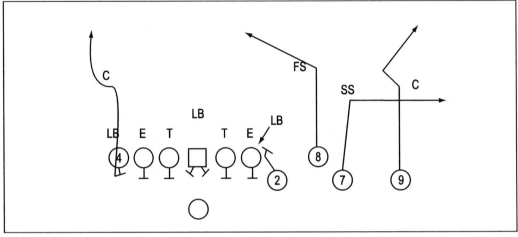

Diagram 7-23

Sprint Out Pass Patterns

Pro Right, Double Slot Left (Diagram 7-24)

Quarterback read:

- Left cornerback throw to 7, 2, or 8

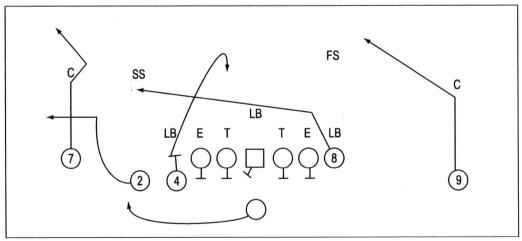

Diagram 7-24

Pro Right, Trips Right, Slot Left (Diagram 7-25)

Quarterback read:

- Right cornerback throw to 9, 4, or 2

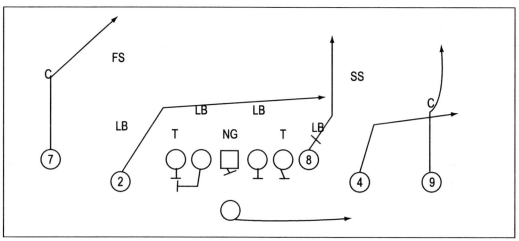

Diagram 7-25

Pro Left, Motion to Trips Left (Diagram 7-26)

Quarterback read:

- Left cornerback throw to 9, 4, or 7

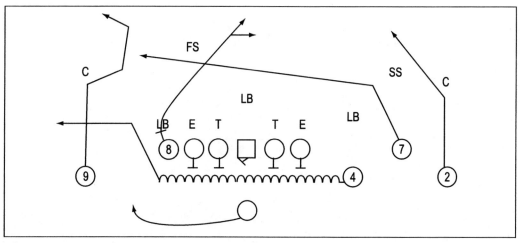

Diagram 7-26

Double Tight, Wing Right (Diagrams 7-27 and 7-28)

Quarterback read:

- Right cornerback throw to 9 or 7
- Free safety throw to 2

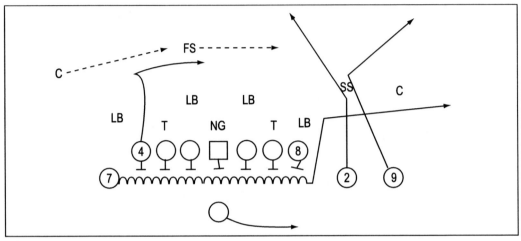

Diagram 7-27

Quarterback read:

- Right cornerback throw to 9, 2, or 8

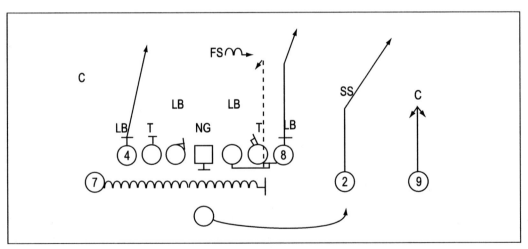

Diagram 7-28

Pro Left, Slot Right Open, Wing (Diagrams 7-29 through 7-33)

Quarterback read:

- Right cornerback throw to 7, 2, or 4

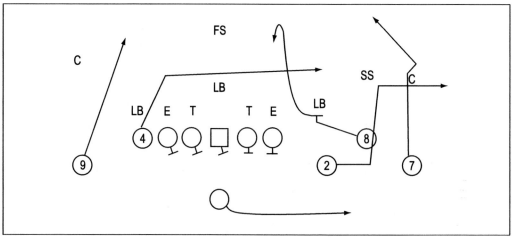

Diagram 7-29

Quarterback read:

- Right cornerback throw to 7 or 9

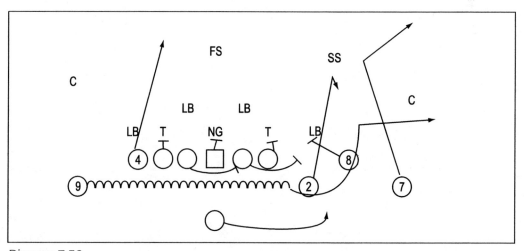

Diagram 7-30

Quarterback read:

- Strong safety throw to 7 or 2
- Right cornerback throw to 7, 9, or 4

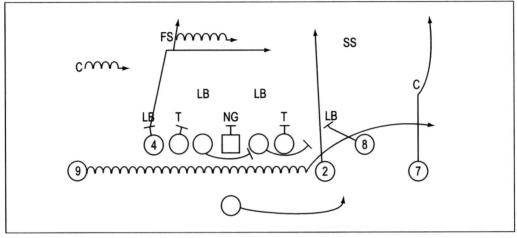

Diagram 7-31

Quarterback read:

- Right cornerback throw to 7 or 2

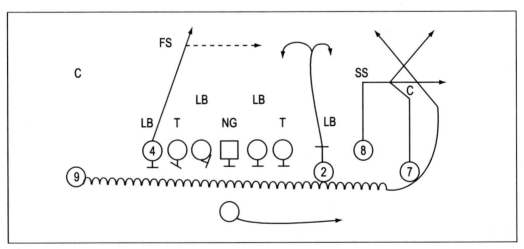

Diagram 7-32

Quarterback read:

- Right cornerback throw to 7 or 8

- Strong safety throw to 8 or 9

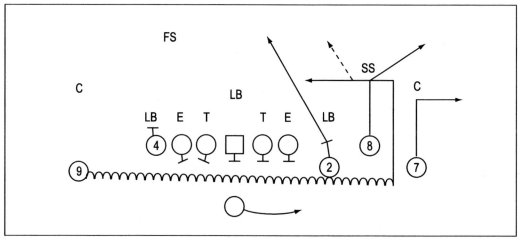

Diagram 7-33

8

Play-Action Passes, Draws, and Screens

The empty backfield passing game would not be complete without a good complement of play-action passes, screens, and draw plays. Play-action passes can be used to take advantage of overanxious defenders intent upon stopping the run. Great run fakes by the quarterback and running backs will sell "run" to the defenders and allow the pass receivers to get open with their pass routes.

Screen plays can be used to take advantage of defenders that are applying a lot of pass rush pressure on the quarterback. The pass fake by the quarterback will draw the pass rushers and/or blitzers to the quarterback and allow the screen receiver to catch the pass and run downfield with releasing linemen blocking on defensive backs.

Draw plays can also be used to take advantage of defenders that are trying to pressure the quarterback into throwing quickly. By faking a pass set-up first, the quarterback will influence the pass rushers to attack the quarterback, rather than playing their run responsibilities. Thus, it allows the draw play runner to run past the pass rushers, and then avoid linebackers and defensive backs that started the play by defending the pass.

Play-Action Passes

Option Play-Action Passes (Diagrams 8-1 through 8-3)

Option Pass or Run

Quarterback read:

- Right cornerback 9 or 8

- Right outside linebacker pitch to 7

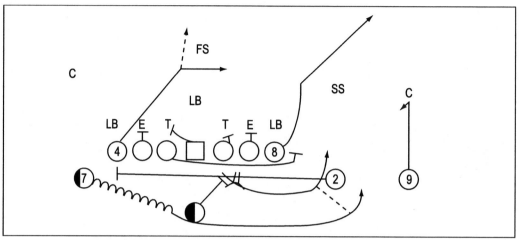

Diagram 8-1. Double tight, wing right

Quarterback read:

- Right cornerback throw to 7 or 2

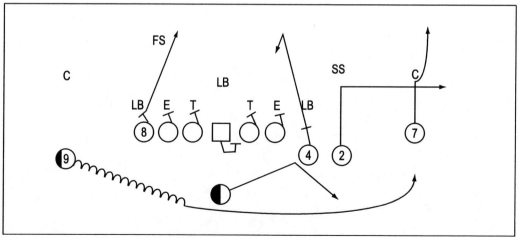

Diagram 8-2. Pro left, double slot right

Option Pass or Run

Quarterback read:

- Right cornerback throw to 9 or 8
- Right outside linebacker pressure—pitch to 2

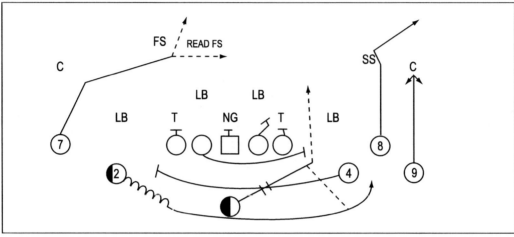

Diagram 8-3. Pro right open, slot left

Fake Counter Play-Action Passes (Diagrams 8-4 through 8-7)

Quarterback read:

- Right cornerback throw to 9 or 7

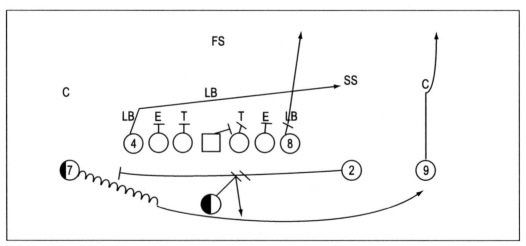

Diagram 8-4

Quarterback read:

- Left cornerback throw to 7 or 4

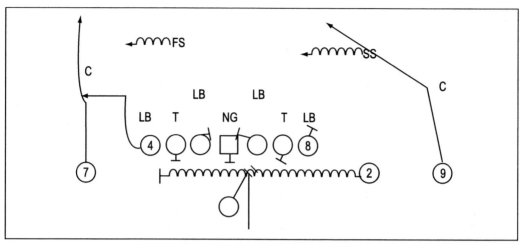

Diagram 8-5. Double tight, wing right

Quarterback read:

- Right cornerback throw to 7 or 8

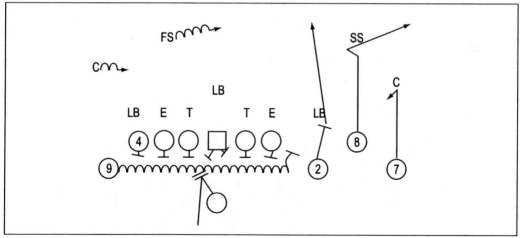

Diagram 8-6. Pro left, slot right open, wing

Quarterback read:

- Strong safety throw to 9 or 8
- Left cornerback throw to 7 or 4

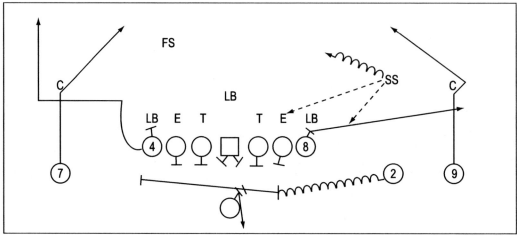

Diagram 8-7. Double tight, wing right

Fake Reverse Play-Action Passes (Diagrams 8-8 through 8-13)

Quarterback read:

- Left cornerback throw to 4, 2, or 9

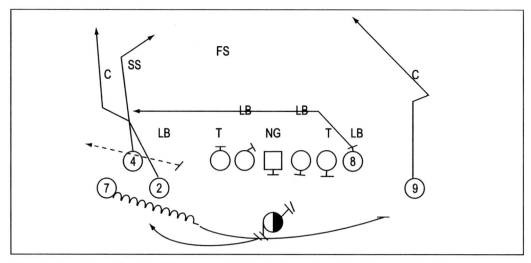

Diagram 8-8. Pro right, slot left open, wing

Note: 7 receives handoff from the quarterback, fakes the reverse, throws back to the quarterback.

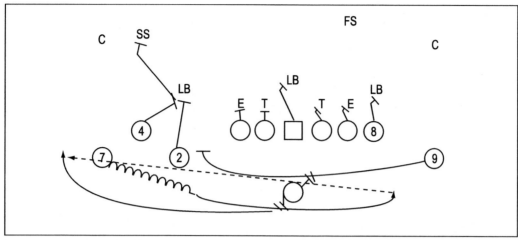

Diagram 8-9. Pro right, slot left open, wing

Note: 9 receives handoff from the quarterback, reads the right cornerback, throws to 7 or 4.

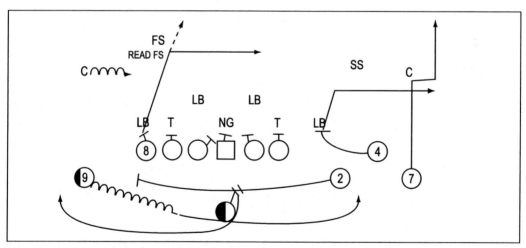

Diagram 8-10. Pro left, slot right open, wing

Quarterback read:

- Strong safety throw to 9 or 8

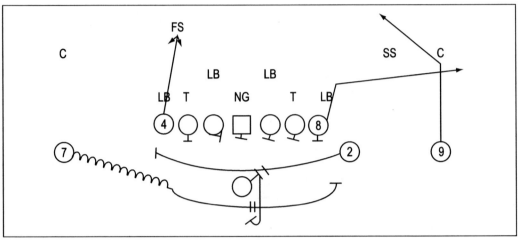

Diagram 8-11. Double tight, wing right

Note: the quarterback fakes handoff to 7; shovel pass to 2

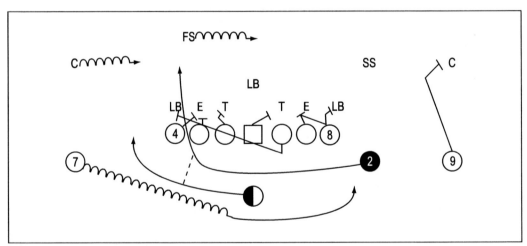

Diagram 8-12. Double tight, wing right

Quarterback read:

- Left cornerback throw to 4 or 2

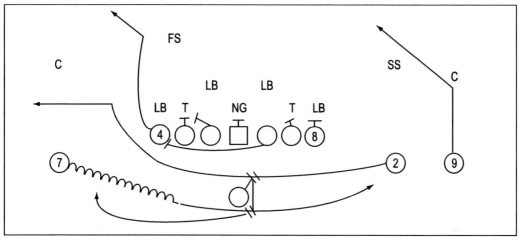

Diagram 8-13

Two Back Middle Screen (Diagram 8-14)

Note:

- All linemen hold their blocks for two seconds before releasing downfield to block.

- The quarterback either throws over or between the rushers. Throw incomplete into the ground if 2 not open.

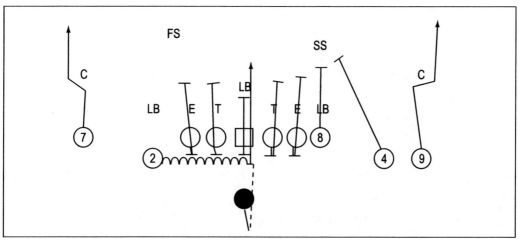

Diagram 8-14. Pro right, trips right, slot left

Four Back Middle Screen (Diagram 8-15)

Note:

- All linemen hold their blocks for two seconds before releasing downfield to block.

- The quarterback either throws over or between the rushers. Throw incomplete into the ground if 4 not open.

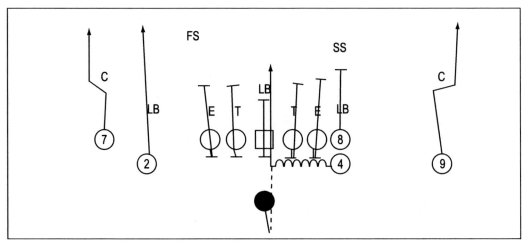

Diagram 8-15. Pro right, trips right, slot left

Nine (Flanker) Screen (Diagram 8-16)

Quarterback read:

- Right outside linebacker throw to 9 or 2

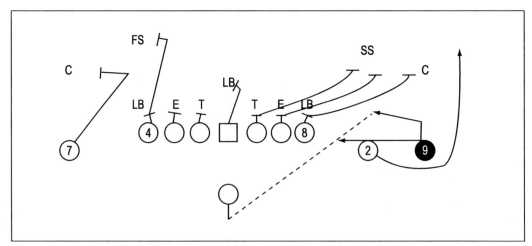

Diagram 8-16. Double tight, wing right

Eight Middle Screen (Diagram 8-17)

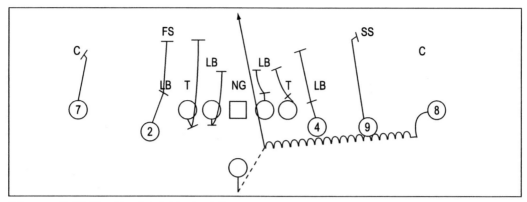

Diagram 8-17. Double slot right, slot left

Two (Motion) Screen Right (Diagram 8-18)

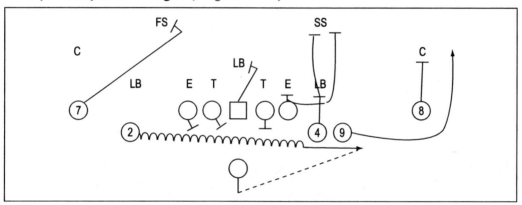

Diagram 8-18. Double slot right, slot left

Four Back Screen Right (Diagram 8-19)

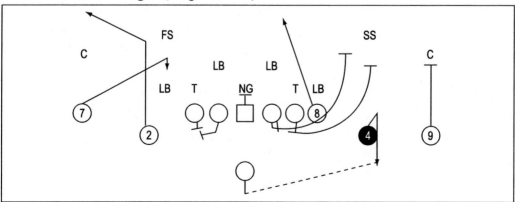

Diagram 8-19. Pro right, trips right, slot left

Eight (Tight End) Screen Left (Diagram 8-20)

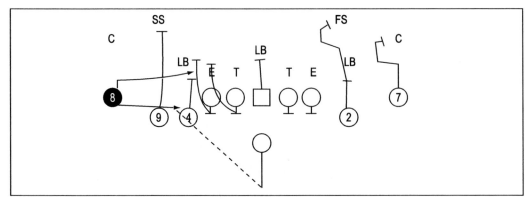

Diagram 8-20. Pro left open, double slot, slot right

Nine (Flanker Motion) Throwback Screen Left (Diagram 8-21)

Note: The quarterback sprints right, then throws back to 9

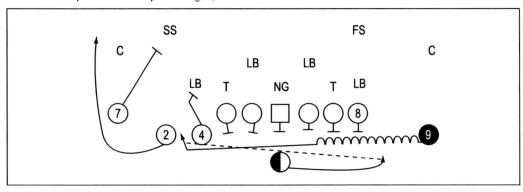

Diagram 8-21. Pro right, double slot left

Draws

Ten Quarterback Draw (Diagram 8-22)

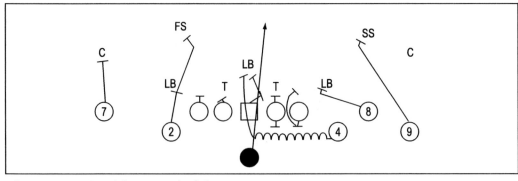

Diagram 8-22. Pro right open, slot left

14 **Quarterback Draw** (Diagram 8-23)

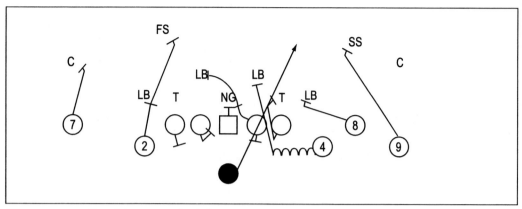

Diagram 8-23. Pro right open, slot left

44 **Draw** (Diagram 8-24)

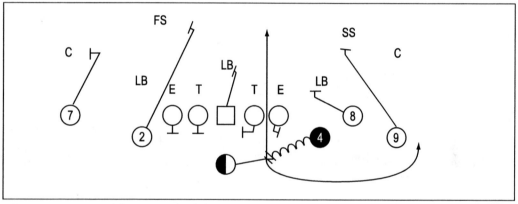

Diagram 8-24. Pro right open, slot left

Note: 9 reads direction of noseguard charge

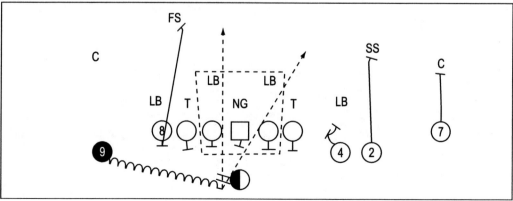

Diagram 8-25. Pro left, double slot right

9

Field Position and Down-and-Distance Strategy

The Red Zone Offense

The playing field inside the 20-yard line is compressed vertically, but not horizontally. Therefore, the empty backfield offense can stretch the pass zones horizontally. However, vertical stretch of the pass zones diminishes as the line of scrimmage gets closer to the goal line. To make up for the shorter vertical field, the following plays can be effective strategies:

- Crossing patterns from one side of the field to the other
- Crossing two receivers aligned near each other or stacked
- Double "in" breaking or double "out" breaking routes
- Sprint out passes
- Screens and draws
- Quarterback options and bootlegs
- Two, three, or four receivers on vertical routes

The offense should anticipate the "box" being loaded with seven or eight potential pass rushers, with corresponding tighter coverage on the receivers. These blitz alignments are fairly common in all field positions versus the empty backfield offense, thus the offense can easily cope with them in the red zone.

Run Plays from the 20-Yard Line to the Eight-Yard Line
(Diagrams 9-1 through 9-7)

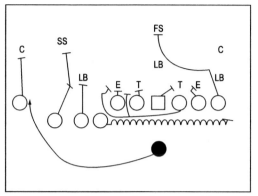

Diagram 9-1. 17 Quarterback sweep (shotgun)

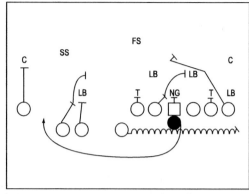

Diagram 9-2. 17 Quarterback sweep

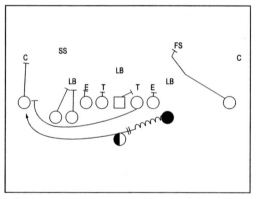

Diagram 9-3. 27 sweep (shotgun)

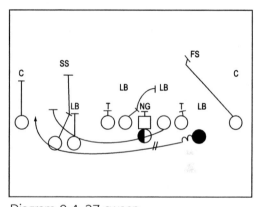

Diagram 9-4. 27 sweep

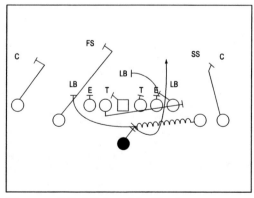

Diagram 9-5. 16 (trap blocking)

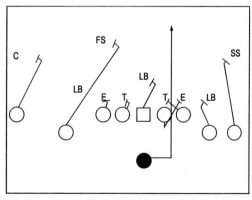

Diagram 9-6. 14 (cross blocking)

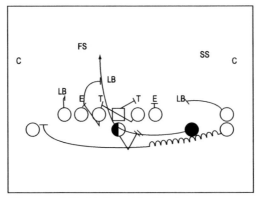

Diagram 9-7. 41 (trap blocking)

Pass Plays from the 20-Yard Line to the Eight-Yard Line

(Diagrams 9-8 through 9-13)

Quarterback read:

- Left cornerback throw to 7, 2, or 8
- Right cornerback throw to 8 or 9
- Strong safety throw to 9 or 8

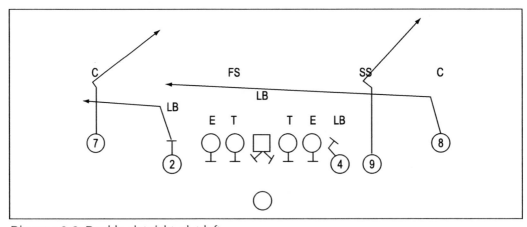

Diagram 9-8. Double slot right, slot left

Quarterback read:

- Right outside linebacker throw to 2 or 8
- Strong safety throw to 8 or 7

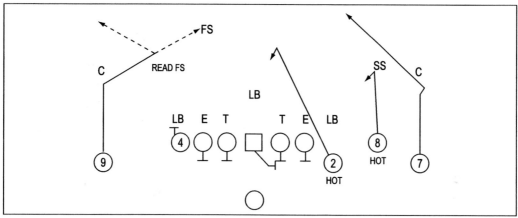

Diagram 9-9. Pro left, slot right open, wing

Quarterback read:

- Left cornerback throw to 9 or 2

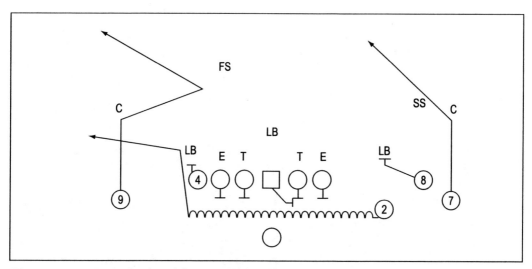

Diagram 9-10. Pro Left, Slot Right Open, Wing

Quarterback read:

- Left cornerback throw to 7 or 2
- Strong safety throw to 9 or 8

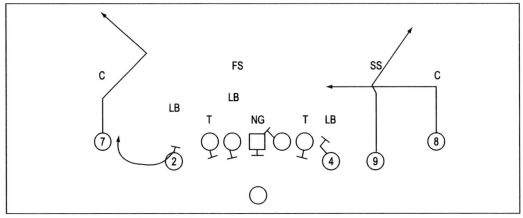

Diagram 9-11. Double slot right, slot left

Quarterback read:

- Left cornerback throw to 9 or 2

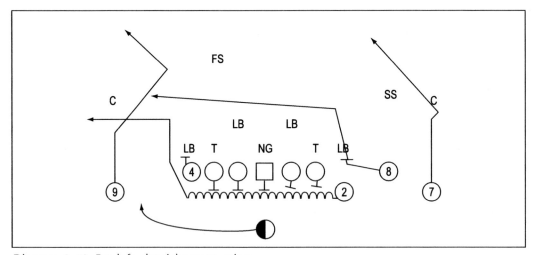

Diagram 9-12. Pro left, slot right open, wing

Quarterback read:

- Right cornerback throw to 9 or 7

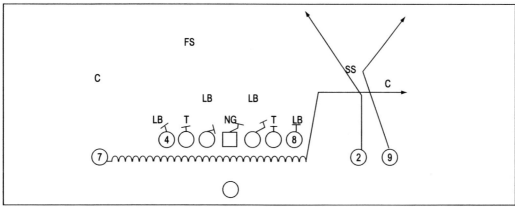

Diagram 9-13. Double tight, wing right

Screens and Draws from the 20-Yard line to the Eight-Yard Line
(Diagrams 9-14 through 9-19)

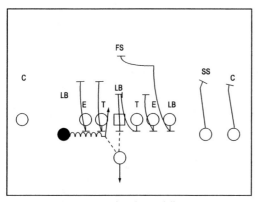

Diagram 9-14. Two back middle screen

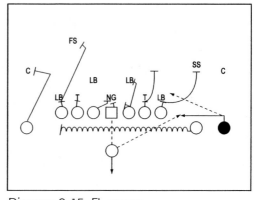

Diagram 9-15. FL screen

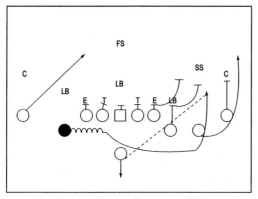

Diagram 9-16. Two back screen right

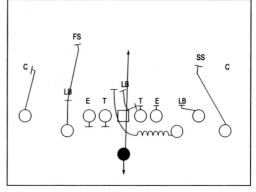

Diagram 9-17. Ten draw

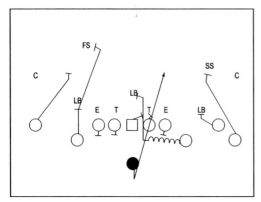

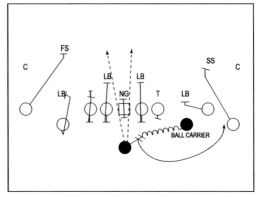

Diagram 9-18. 14 draw   Diagram 9-19. 40 draw

Offense from the Eight-Yard Line to the Goal Line

As the offense gets closer to the goal line, the defense will tighten their coverage on the receivers and play their defensive backs on the goal line. The defense will also try to apply more pressure on the quarterback with blitzes and man-to-man coverage. Because the field is compressed vertically even more, the offense must be creative in pass patterns that allow the quarterback to throw quickly. "Bunching" three or four receivers to one side will probably force zone coverage and thus create some "windows" for the quarterback to throw into the end zone.

Run Plays from the Eight-Yard Line to the Goal Line (Diagrams 9-20 through 9-25)

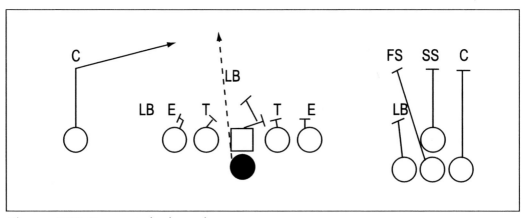

Diagram 9-20. Ten quarterback sneak

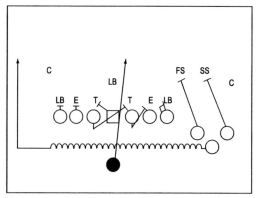

Diagram 9-21. Ten (trap blocking)

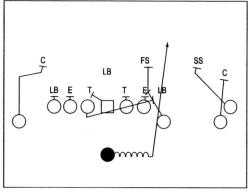

Diagram 9-22. 16 (trap blocking)

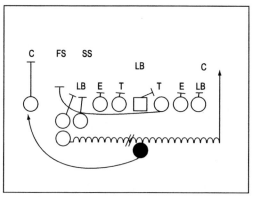

Diagram 9-23. 17 sweep

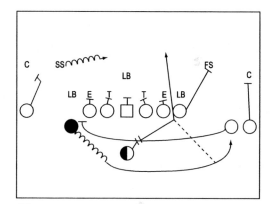

Diagram 9-24. 18 option

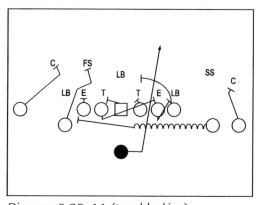

Diagram 9-25. 14 (trap blocking)

Pass Plays from the Eight-Yard Line to the Goal Line (Diagram 9-26 through 9-29)

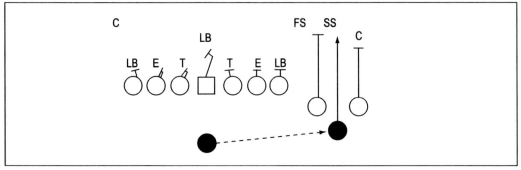

Diagram 9-26. Bunch right, spot pass

Quarterback read:

- Right cornerback throw to 9, 2, or 7

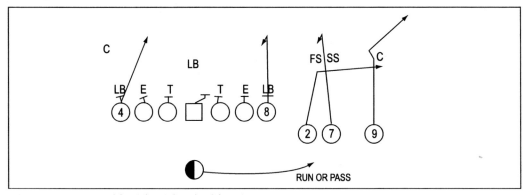

Diagram 9-27. Double tight right, double wing

Quarterback read:

- Right cornerback throw to 7 or 2

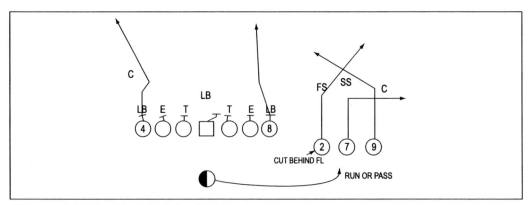

Diagram 9-28. Double tight right, double wing

Quarterback read:

• Free safety throw to 2 or 9

Note: If free safety is head up or outside, 2-back will post. If free safety is inside, 2-back will flag.

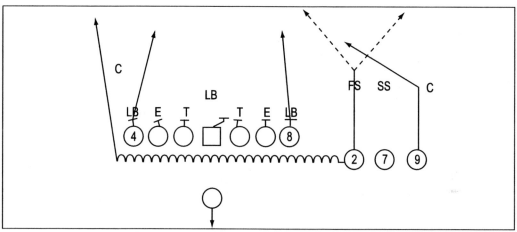

Diagram 9-29. Double tight right, double wing

Play-Action Pass Plays from the Eight-Yard Line to the Goal Line
(Diagrams 9-30 through 9-35)

Quarterback read:

• Fake to 4-back; throw to 2 or 9

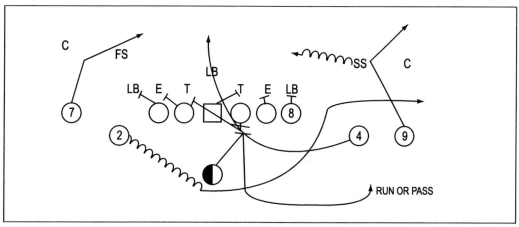

Diagram 9-30. Pro right, trips right, slot left

Quarterback read:

* Fake to 2-back; throw to 2, 9, or 7

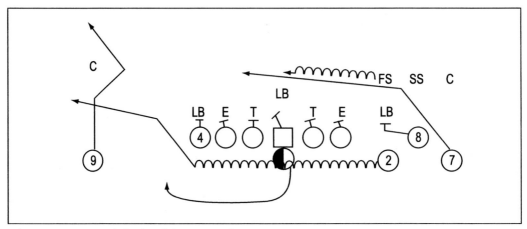

Diagram 9-31. Pro left, slot right open, wing

Quarterback read:

* Sprint right; throw to 7, 9, or 2

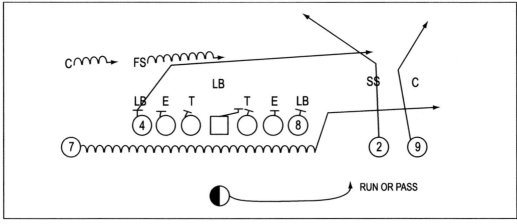

Diagram 9-32. Double tight, wing right

Quarterback read:

- Throw to either side

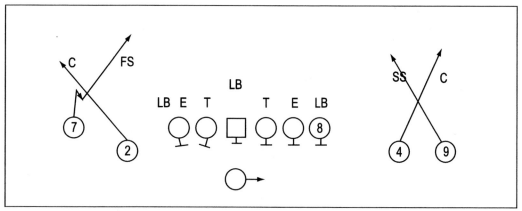

Diagram 9-33. Pro right, trips right, slot left

Quarterback read:

- Cornerback inside; throw to 9 or 7
- Strong safety outside; throw to 4 or 2

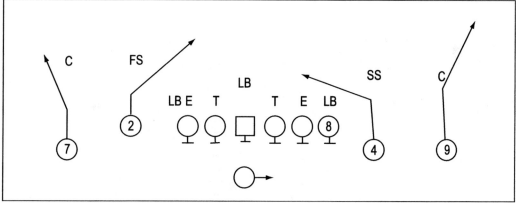

Diagram 9-34. Pro right, trips right, slot left

Quarterback read:

- Right cornerback throw to 8 or 9
- Left cornerback throw to 7 or 2

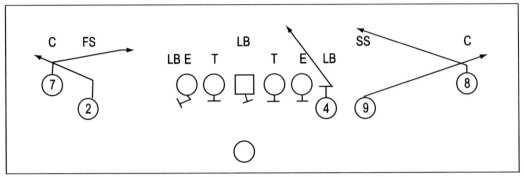

Diagram 9-35. Pro right open, double slot, slot left

Down-and Distance-Considerations

Down-and-distance considerations are often of lesser importance with the empty backfield offense than the defensive alignment. Of course, exceptions exist, but answering the following questions is more important in play selection:

- Is the strength of the defense versus run or pass?
- Is the defense vulnerable to a "hot" or audible call?
- Do personnel mismatches exist?
- How many defensive linemen and linebackers versus defensive backs?

Short Yardage Situations

The conventional defensive approach to short yardage situations is to place six defenders in the "box" and play man-to-man pass defense on the receivers. (Diagrams 9-36 and 9-37)

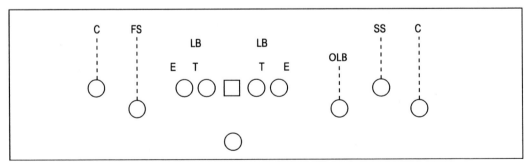

Diagram 9-36. Four defensive backs, three linebackers, four defensive linemen

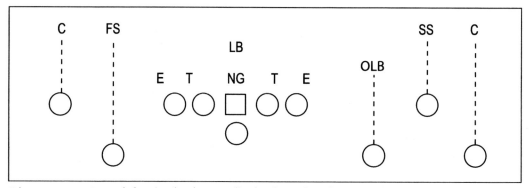

Diagram 9-37. Four defensive backs, two linebackers, five defensive linemen

This alignment is strong against the run, but may break down on pass coverage if the quarterback has time to throw. The defense can also blitz one or two linebackers from these alignments. (Diagrams 9-38 through 9-40)

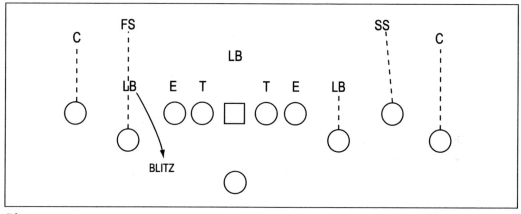

Diagram 9-38

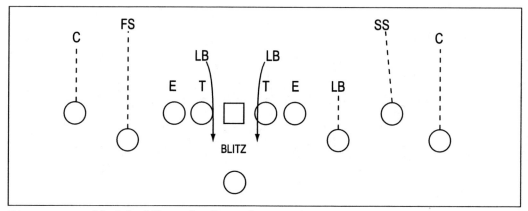

Diagram 9-39 (block "solid" on all split LB alignments)

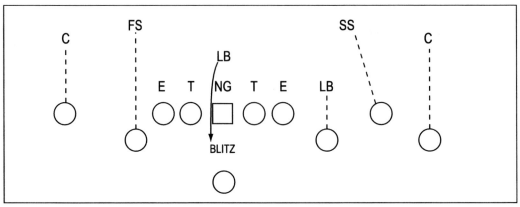

Diagram 9-40. "Block solid"

Long Yardage Situations

The conventional defensive approach to long yardage situations is to replace either defensive linemen or linebackers with extra defensive backs (Diagrams 9-41 through 9-43). This strategy is intended to strengthen the pass defense, but may weaken the run defense. Even though this strategy seems strong versus the pass, it is still difficult to play zone effectively against the empty backfield offense. When playing zones versus the five wide receiver formations, the defensive secondary gets spread both horizontally and vertically, which creates large open areas.

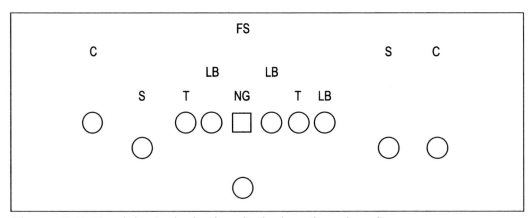

Diagram 9-41. Five defensive backs, three linebackers, three down linemen

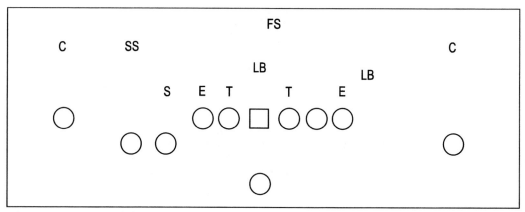

Diagram 9-42. Five defensive backs, two linebackers, four defensive linemen

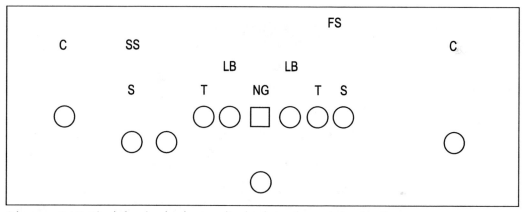

Diagram 9-43. Six defensive backs, two linebackers, three defensive linemen

10

Pre-Reading Defenses

Pre-reading defensive alignments requires all offensive players to become aware of what defenses can do from certain alignments, as well as the strengths and weaknesses of these alignments. This information must be mentally processed in the few seconds between the time the offense sets at the line of scrimmage and the snap of the ball. In order to make an accurate assessment, the offensive players should be taught defensive alignments and responsibilities.

General Guidelines

If the defense is using multiple fronts and coverages, the offense can use the "check with me" play calling system. In the huddle, the quarterback will call a formation and the snap count, and then say, "Check with me." Once aligned at the line of scrimmage, the quarterback will pre-read the defense and call a play to attack that particular defense.

If the defense is using four defensive backs, the offense can use formations with three receivers to one side. To cover the middle pass zone with one or two safeties, the defense will need to move a linebacker to the three receiver side, thus weakening inside run support and possibly forcing the outside linebackers to cover a receiver or pass (Diagram 10-1). To cover the three receivers with defensive backs, the defense must move a safety from the middle, thus becoming vulnerable to deep middle pass routes and forcing an outside linebacker to cover a receiver or pass (Diagram 10-2). If the defense "stacks" linebackers or defensive backs either behind or between defensive linemen, the offense should be alert for blitz. (Diagram 10-3)

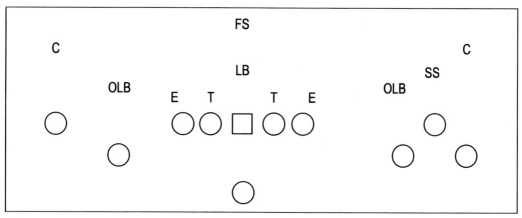

Diagram 10-1

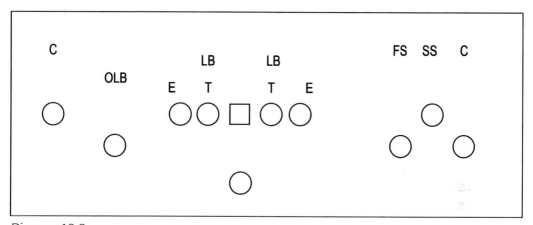

Diagram 10-2

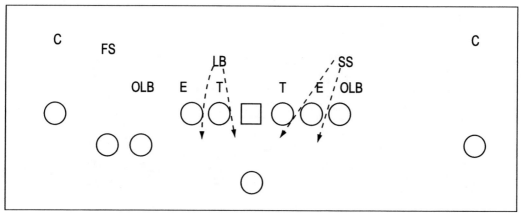

Diagram 10-3

If the defense is playing either a two-deep or three-deep zone, with man-to-man coverage on the receivers, they must remove a linebacker from the box. Thus, they are vulnerable to the inside run. (Diagrams 10-4 and 10-5).

Pre-Reading the Empty Backfield Formations

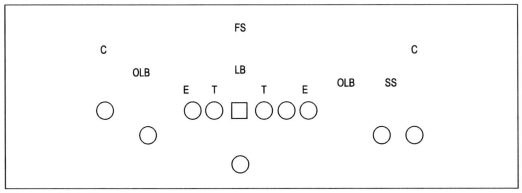

Diagram 10-4. Three-deep zone

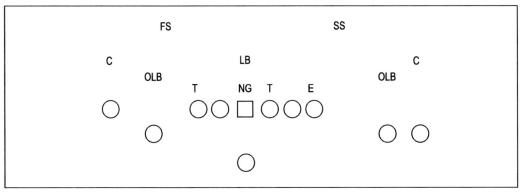

Diagram 10-5. Two-deep zone

Formation 1: Pro Right, Double Slot Left (Diagrams 10-6 through 10-11)

Note:

- A mismatch in pass coverage exists on the left side.

- Good blocking angles exist at the 5 and 6 holes.

- Cross block the 0, 3, and 4 holes.

- Run stretch and sweep plays at the 8 hole.

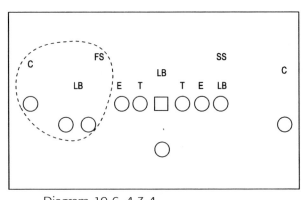

Diagram 10-6. 4-3-4

Note:

- A mismatch in pass coverage exists on the left side.

- Run outside versus the six defenders between the tackles.

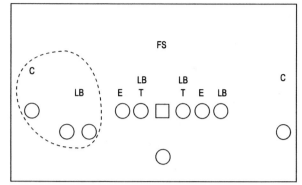

Diagram 10-7. 4-4-3

Note:

- A mismatch in pass coverage exists on the left side.

- Good blocking angles exist at the 5 and 6 holes.

- Cross block the 0, 3, and 4 holes.

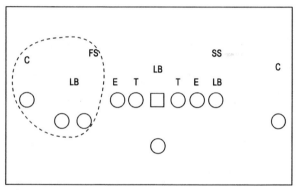

Diagram 10-8. 4-3-4

Note:

- A mismatch in pass coverage exists on the left side.

- Good blocking angles exist at the 5 and 6 holes.

- Run, stretch, and sweep plays at the 8 hole.

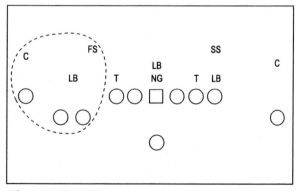

Diagram 10-9. 3-4-4

Note:

- A mismatch in pass coverage exists on the left side.

- Good blocking angles exist at the 5 and 6 holes.

- Cross and trap block the 3 and 4 holes.

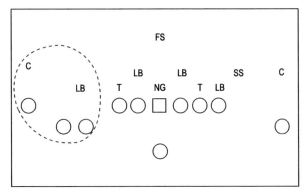

Diagram 10-10. 3-5-3

Note:

- The extra safeties dictate run.

- Run at the extra safeties in the 7 and 8 holes.

- A mismatch in pass coverage exists on the left side.

Note: Two extra safeties have replaced the outside linebackers.

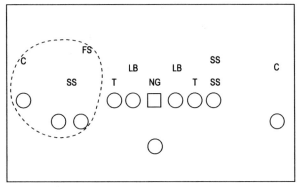

Diagram 10-11. 3-4-4

Formation 2: Pro Right, Trips Right, Slot Left (Diagrams 10-2 through 10-17)

Note:

- A mismatch in pass coverage exists on the right side.

- The 7 hole is outflanked, thus vulnerable to the run.

- Good blocking angles exist at the 5 and 6 holes.

- Cross block the 0, 3, and 4 holes.

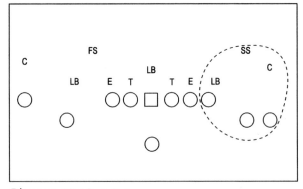

Diagram 10-12. 4-3-4

Note:

- The secondary is short defenders, thus look for the blitz.

- A mismatch in pass coverage exists on both sides.

- Run outside versus the six defenders between the tackles.

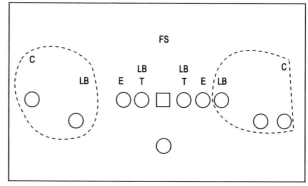

Diagram 10-13. 4-4-3

Note:

- The extra safeties dictate run.

- Run at the extra safeties in the 7 and 8 holes.

- Cross block the 0, 3, and 4 holes.

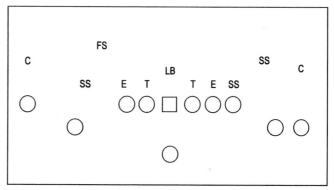

Diagram 10-14. 4-3-4

Note:

- A mismatch in pass coverage exists on the right side.

- Good blocking angles exist at the 5 and 6 holes.

- Cross block and trap the 3 and 4 holes.

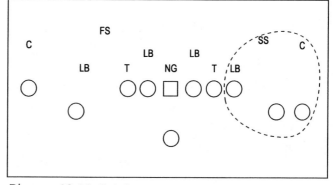

Diagram 10-15. 3-4-4

Note:

- A mismatch exists on the right side unless the free safety moves to the tight end side.

- Run inside the tackles because the defense only has one inside linebacker.

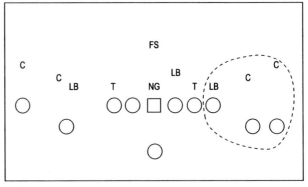

Diagram 10-16. 3-3-5

Note:

- The extra safeties dictate run.

- Run at the safeties in the 7 and 8 holes.

Note: Two extra safeties have replaced the outside linebackers.

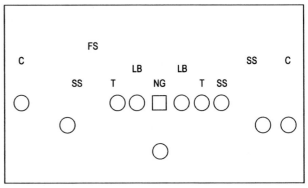

Diagram 10-17. 3-4-4

Formation 3: Pro Left, Slot Right Open, Wing (Diagrams 10-18 through 10-23)

Note:

- A mismatch in pass coverage exists on the right side (linebacker in coverage of wide receiver).

- Good blocking angles exist at the 5 and 6 holes.

- Cross block the 0, 3, and 4 holes.

- Run stretch play at the 7 hole.

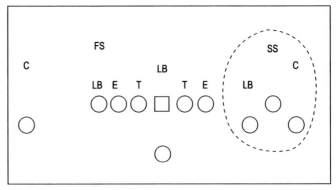

Diagram 10-18. 4-3-4

Note:

- A mismatch in pass coverage exists on both sides.

- Run outside versus the six defenders between the tackles.

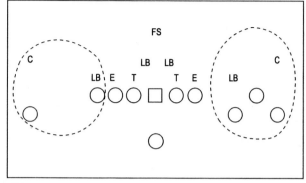

Diagram 10-19. 4-4-3

Note:

- A mismatch in pass coverage exists on the right side.

- Run at the safeties in the 7 and 8 holes.

Note: Two extra safeties have replaced the outside linebackers.

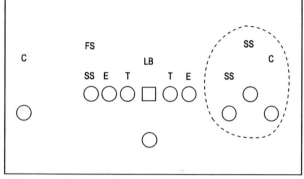

Diagram 10-20. 4-3-4

Note:

- A mismatch in pass coverage exists on the right side.

- Run stretch and sweep plays at the 7 and 8 holes.

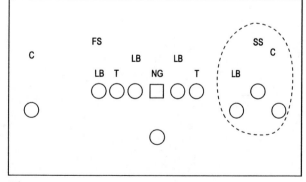

Diagram 10-21. 3-4-4

Note:

- A mismatch in pass coverage exists on the right side.

- Run inside the tackles because the defense only has one inside linebacker.

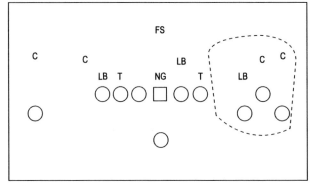

Diagram 10-22. 3-3-5

Note:

- A mismatch in pass coverage exists on the right side.

- Run at the extra safeties in the 7 and 8 holes.

Note: Two extra safeties have replaced the outside linebackers.

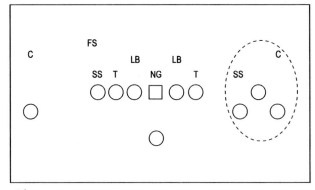

Diagram 10-23. 3-6-2

Formation 4: Double Tight, Wing Right (Diagrams 10-24 through 10-28)

Note:

- A mismatch in pass coverage exists on the left side, unless the free safety moves to that side.

- A mismatch in pass coverage exists with linebackers covering receivers.

- Run to the left side.

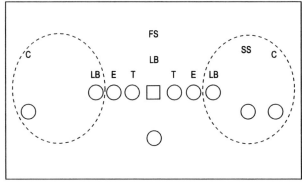

Diagram 10-24. 4-3-4

Note:

- A mismatch in pass coverage exists on both sides.

- Run outside versus the six defenders between the tackles.

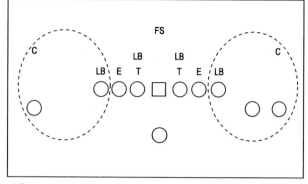

Diagram 10-25. 4-4-3

Note:

- A mismatch in pass coverage exists on the right side.

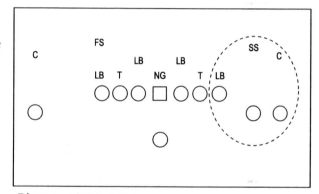

Diagram 10-26. 3-4-4

Note:

- A mismatch in pass coverage exists on the right side.

- Run inside the tackles because the defense only has one inside linebacker.

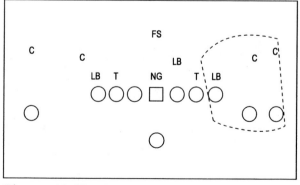

Diagram 10-27. 3-3-5

Note:

- A mismatch in pass coverage exists on the right side.

- Run at the safeties in the 7 and 8 holes.

Note: Two extra safeties have replaced the outside linebackers.

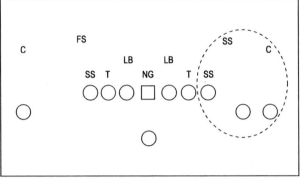

Diagram 10-28. 3-4-4

Formations 5 and 6: Pro Right Open, Slot Left and Pro Right Open, Wing, Slot Left (Diagrams 10-29 through 10-34)

Note:

- A mismatch in pass coverage exists on the right side.

- Run inside because the outside linebackers are in pass coverage alignments.

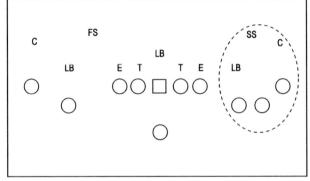

Diagram 10-29. 4-3-4

Note:

- A mismatch in pass coverage exists on both sides.

- Run outside versus the six defenders between the tackles.

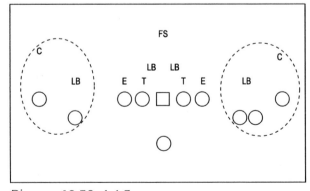

Diagram 10-30. 4-4-3

Note:

- A mismatch in pass coverage exists on the left side.

- Run inside because the safeties are in pass coverage alignments.

- Run at the extra safeties.

Note: Two extra safeties have replaced the outside linebackers.

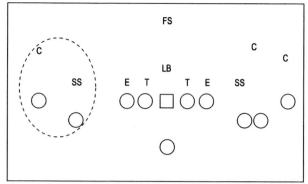

Diagram 10-31. 4-3-4

Note:

- A mismatch in pass coverage exists on the right side.

- Be alert for blitz on the left side if the free safety moves over to the slot.

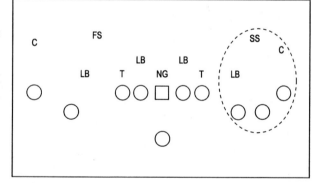

Diagram 10-32. 3-4-4

Note:

- A mismatch in pass coverage exists on the right side unless the free safety moves over to the double-slot side.

- Run inside because the outside linebackers are in pass coverage alignments.

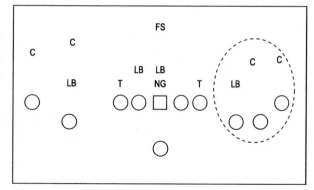

Diagram 10-33. 3-3-5

Note:

- A mismatch in pass coverage exists on the left side unless the free safety moves over to the slot.

- Run outside at the extra safeties.

Note: Two extra safeties have replaced the outside linebackers.

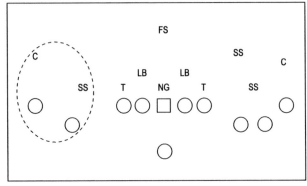

Diagram 10-34. 3-4-4

Formation 7: Double Tight Right, Double Wing (Diagrams 10-35 through 10-37)

Note:

- The pass coverage alignment dictates zone.

- Run outside to the left side.

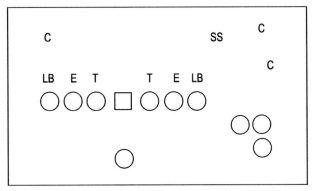

Diagram 10-35. 4-3-4

Note:

- A mismatch in pass coverage exists on the right side.

- Run outside versus the six defenders between the tackles.

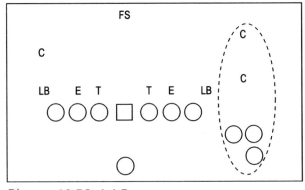

Diagram 10-36. 4-4-3

Note:

- A mismatch in pass coverage exists on the right side.

- Run at the extra safeties in the 7 and 8 holes.

Note: Two extra safeties have replaced the outside linebackers.

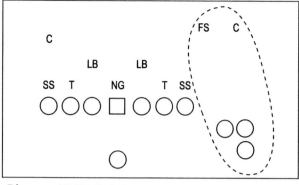

Diagram 10-37. 3-4-4

Formation 8: Pro Right Open, Slot Stack, Backside Tight (Diagrams 10-38 through 10-40)

Note:

- A mismatch in pass coverage exists on the right side.

- Run outside at the 7 and 8 holes.

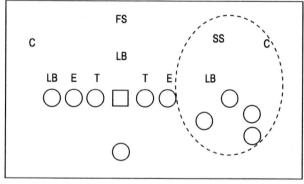

Diagram 10-38. 4-3-4

Note:

- A mismatch in pass coverage exists on the right side.

- Run outside versus the six defenders between the tackles.

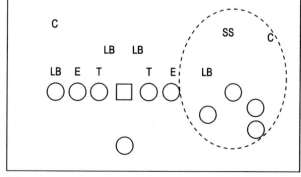

Diagram 10-39. 4-4-3

Note:

- A mismatch in pass coverage occurs unless the free safety moves over to the slot stack side.

- Run at the extra safeties in the 7 and 8 holes.

Note: Two extra safeties have replaced the outside linebackers.

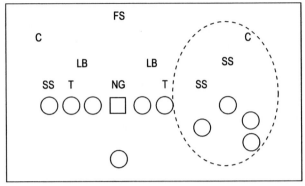

Diagram 10-40. 3-4-4

Glossary

Abbreviations

BC	Ballcarrier	**NG**	Nose Guard	**LCB**	Left Cornerback
LOS	Line of Scrimmage	**E**	Defensive End	**RSS**	Right Strong Safety
SE	Split End	**LB**	Linebacker	**LSS**	Left Strong Safety
TE	Tight End	**LOLB**	Left Outside Linebacker	**FS**	Free Safety
FL	Flanker	**ROLB**	Right Outside Linebacker	**SS**	Strong Safety
QB	Quarterback	**MLB**	Middle Linebacker		
T	Defensive Tackle	**RCB**	Right Cornerback		

Terminology

Blitzing	a linebacker rushing the passer
Come	a linebacker blitzing
Fly	a receiver running a deep route straight down the field
Slot	a receiver, off the LOS, between two other offensive players
Scheme	a group of movements all designed to accomplish one goal
Pre-read	to scan the defensive alignment immediately prior to the snap of the ball and tentatively anticipate the offensive possibility
Pro	an offensive formation based on the appearance of a tight end
Audible	the changing of a play at the LOS that was previous called in the huddle
Hot	a receiver designated to be the pass target when the offensive anticipates either an overload or a blitz
Stretch	an offensive play wherein the blockers take the defenders in the direction the defender wants to go and the BC finds a hole or running lane wherever he can go
Alignment	the position a group of offensive or defensive players occupy
Red Zone	the area from the 20-yard line into the goal line
Empty Backfield	alignment with only one offensive player from tackle to tackle
Stacks	when two or more players are aligned either behind each other or in gaps between two players
Automatic	a pre-determined play based on something the defense does
Loaded Side	a side, from the center, where more defenders than normal line up
Defender "Disappearing"	a defender, usually a defensive back, who leaves his original position to blitz or confuse the passer

About the Author

A native of Steubenville, Ohio, Joe Gilliam, Sr. is one of the most respected coaches in the history of the game. He began his intercollegiate football career at Indiana University, where he played on the Hoosiers' national championship football team. He then went into the Armed Services, and upon his discharge, enrolled at West Virginia State College, where he played both basketball and football. At West Virginia State College, he received All-American honors as a quarterback and earned a place in the Yellow Jackets' Sports Hall of Fame.

Coach Gilliam began his 35-year coaching career on the high school level in Kentucky, where he earned the Kentucky High School Football Association's Coach of the Year title. He went on to coach on the collegiate level at Jackson State College in Mississippi, helping lead the Tigers to the National Black Championship title.

From 1963-1981, Gilliam was the assistant head football coach and defensive coordinator for Tennessee State University. In 1989, he took the helm as head coach for four seasons. During this time, he was inducted into the TSU Sports Hall of Fame, and was selected as Coach of the Year in the Ohio Valley Conference in 1990. His illustrious career record of 254-93-15 included coaching five undefeated teams and five other teams that lost only one game. In the process, he coached ten teams to national championships, and helped guide 144 players into professional football careers with the National Football League. Most recently, he worked with the Arizona Cardinals' coaching staff as an offensive consultant during the summer. Gilliam currently conducts a summer football camp for underprivileged children in Nashville, Tennessee.

Throughout his extensive career, Gilliam has earned numerous awards, including the All-American Football Foundation Lifetime Achievement Award and the College Football Hall of Fame Contribution Award. A frequent guest speaker and sought-after lecturer at football clinics, radio programs, and sports banquets, he is widely renowned for the ability of his teams to employ his innovative offensive concepts and insights.